RECIPES INTO TYPE

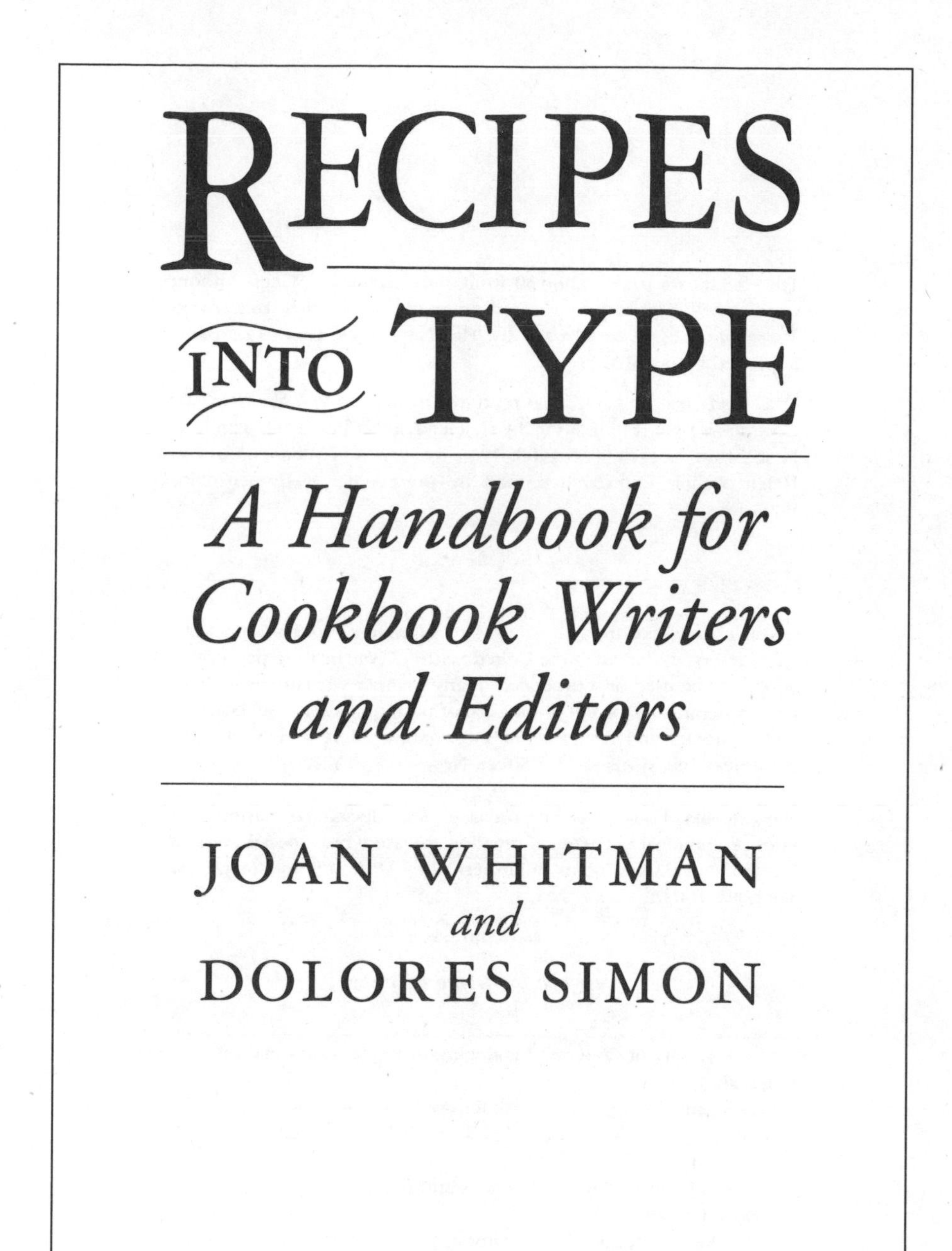

RECIPES INTO TYPE

A Handbook for Cookbook Writers and Editors

JOAN WHITMAN
and
DOLORES SIMON

HarperCollins*Publishers*

HarperCollins books may be purchased for educational, business, or sales promotional use. For information, please write: Special Markets Department, HarperCollins Publishers, Inc., 10 East 53rd Street, New York, NY 10022.

FIRST EDITION

Designed by Helene Berinsky

Library of Congress Cataloging-in-Publication Data

Whitman, Joan.

Recipes into type : a handbook for cookbook writers and editors / Joan Whitman and Dolores Simon.—1st ed.

p. cm.

Includes bibliographical references and index.

ISBN 0-06-270034-0

1. Cookery—Authorship. I. Simon, Dolores, date– II. Title.

TX644.W47 1993

808'.066641—dc20 89-46129

93 94 95 96 97 CC/HC 10 9 8 7 6 5 4 3 2 1

Contents

Preface

THIS STYLEBOOK IS for those who write and edit recipes for publication—specifically for cookbooks but also for pamphlets, for newspapers and periodicals, for collections for fund-raisers, and for marketing and promotional materials. There are several good general stylebooks (this is only a supplement to those), but they do not address the very specific problems of careful recipe writing.

Style, as in *stylebook,* can distinguish a good food writer from a careless one. It concerns the language special to recipes and the acceptable conventions of grammar, punctuation, and capitalization as they apply. It does not refer to literary style, a writer's distinctive way of expressing himself. And there is certainly not just one style for recipe writing.

The proliferation of cookbooks over the last three decades has been nothing short of phenomenal. At the same time there has been increased space in magazines and newspapers allotted to food coverage (except perhaps during a recession). But many excellent cooks are inarticulate writers, and many excellent writers do not understand the intricacies of cooking. The person who is master of both these crafts is a treasure.

An editor is invaluable to any writer, and a good food editor is the key to clearly written recipes. This editor's job is to suggest ways to clarify and improve the text and to make the recipes consistent in wording and format. If the writer has prepared the recipes carefully—anticipating the questions of the person who is to follow them—then the editor's job is much simpler. But the editor should also be knowledgeable about cooking and query anything that is ambiguous.

In *Recipes into Type* we have tried to establish standards of styling and handling that any food writer or editor can follow. We have consulted many widely respected sources in formulating our recommendations, and we bring many years of personal experience to the job as well—Dolores Simon at Harper & Row for thirty-two years, twenty-five of them as chief copy editor, and Joan Whitman at *The New York Times* for twenty-two years, seventeen of them as deputy editor and editor of the family/style pages.

Some of the information in this book concerns cookbook writers and editors, but most of it is about writing and editing recipes for any medium.

RECIPES INTO TYPE

—1—

Setting Up a Recipe

A RECIPE MAY BE INFORMALLY DEFINED as a formula or written set of instructions for preparing food. Although recipes range from simple to extremely complex, most of them contain some or all of the following elements:

Title: A descriptive name assigned to a particular dish.

Headnote: A sentence or paragraph describing the particular merits or peculiarities of the recipe that follows, or giving an anecdote about it.

Ingredients List: A list preceding the instructions that enumerates, in order of their use, the ingredients and quantities that will be needed.

Instructions: Detailed directions, preferably in short paragraphs, on how to prepare and assemble the ingredients to create the desired dish.

Servings Line (Yield Line): A brief (two or three words) statement on how many servings the recipe may be expected to yield.

Note: A sentence or paragraph at the end of a recipe giving additional information about an ingredient or a procedure.

Variation: A suggestion on how to vary a recipe by substituting different ingredients or using a different procedure. The variation follows the note, if any, and in some cases may have a title of its own.

— Title —

The title tells the reader immediately whether to look further into the recipe. It should be inviting and can even have a little romance, but above all it should be informative.

In choosing a title, the food writer should strive for something that is relatively short as well as restrained in the use of adjectives, people's names, and homey or cute words. For those who have been writing recipes for years, it may seem pedestrian to call something "Chicken with Puréed Leeks," but think of the cook thumbing through the book. That title is descriptive and tells him what he wants to know.

Two titles that lean toward the cute but are appealing are Julia Child's "Canned Consommé Dissembled" and James Beard's "My Clam Soup That Cures." But recipe titles should be about food, not mood. Consider the following titles that unfortunately appeared in print:

DREAMS DO COME TRUE
(veal kidneys and chicken livers with mustard, curry, and cream)

BETTER THAN SEX CAKE
(Cool Whip, crushed pineapple, Duncan Hines cake mix)

GREAT AUNT NELLIE'S LEMON SLICES
(shortbread baked with a topping of lemon curd)

Think also of how the title will be indexed, because it should be easy for the reader to find. If there are too many adjectives, proper names, or cute words in the title, the index will be ineffective. How is the cook to locate veal kidneys or pineapple cake or shortbread if it is indexed under "Dreams," "Better," or "Great"? And when recipe titles are very long, the index will be full of turnovers (running over to the next line), which lengthens the index needlessly.

BE INFORMATIVE

There is nothing wrong with playing it straight and telling what is in the recipe.

POOR: Chicken à la Mary
GOOD: Chicken and Sausage Casserole

POOR: Stuffed Onions
GOOD: Onions Stuffed with Curried Lamb

POOR: Tomato Delight
GOOD: Mushroom Pâté in Tomato Shells

POOR: Slam-Bang Beans
GOOD: Spicy Bean Salad

POOR: Red on Red
GOOD: Red Potato and Beet Salad

POOR: Milwaukee Specials
GOOD: Scallion Pancakes

THE AMOS 'N ANDY SYNDROME

Do not try to make a title more appealing or homey by using colloquial English. It may repel rather than attract a reader.

POOR: Chips 'n Granola Bars
GOOD: Chips and Granola Bars

POOR: Cracklin' Good Chicken Wings
GOOD: Deep-fried Chicken Wings

POOR: Bits o' Honey Cake
GOOD: Honey Cake

Such usage in commercial products (Shake 'n Bake, Dunkin' Donuts) is for the purpose of establishing a brand name, and in some cases (Finger-Lickin' Good) an advertising slogan. The food writer can best establish his own good name by using proper English.

FOREIGN WORDS

Foreign words in recipe titles have their place, but they must be carefully chosen. In recipes for unsophisticated beginners, it seems foolish and pretentious to call something "Zuppa di Lenticchie" instead of "Lentil Soup," or "suprême de volaille" instead of "chicken breast." But if the food writer is aiming at a more experienced readership, foreign words are familiar and sometimes add charm. To many writers, "ris de veau" is more appealing than "sweetbreads," and "fruits de mer" is more poetic than "shellfish."

Ideally, both an English title and a foreign title should be given.

Translations

When using foreign recipe titles, translate them in subtitles, and do it descriptively rather than literally.

FEGATO ALLA VENEZIANA

POOR: (Liver Venetian style)

GOOD: (Julienne strips of liver with onions)

POLLO FRA DIAVOLO

POOR: (Deviled chicken)

GOOD: (Spicy baked chicken)

HUEVOS À LA MADRILEÑA

POOR: (Eggs in the style of Madrid)

GOOD: (Baked eggs with sliced tomato and sausage)

ÉMINCÉ DE VEAU À LA ZURICHOISE

POOR: (Minced veal Zurich style)

GOOD: (Veal strips with mushrooms and cream)

When the authentic foreign title is unfamiliar to the reader, as with these Indian ones, it is perhaps more helpful to give the main title in English, with the authentic title in parentheses:

FRIED LENTIL WAFERS
(Papad-Tala)

ZUCCHINI AND YOGURT SALAD
(Pachadi Vallerika)

Classic Terms

There are classic French terms for hundreds of dishes, and for the knowledgeable they serve as a kind of shorthand to describe the ingredients. *Larousse Gastronomique* and *Le Répertoire de la Cuisine,* both valuable books in a reference library, describe these in detail.

But if recipes are aimed at a general audience, shorthand is not a virtue and can intimidate a new generation of cooks who may never have heard of Escoffier, much less the following: *lyonnaise,* for example, means a dish with onions; *Normande,* one with cream, apples, and cider or Calvados; *liégeoise,* one with juniper berries.

The classic title can be either the main title or the subtitle.

SOLE GRENOBLOISE
(Sautéed Sole with Capers and Lemon)

VEAL CHOPS WITH CAULIFLOWER
(Côtes de Veau du Barry)

Mixing Languages

When foreign words are used, it is preferable to make the whole title foreign with a translation, or to use just the English translation.

POOR: Chicken à l'Estragon
GOOD: Poulet à l'Estragon
GOOD: Chicken with Tarragon

Agreement

In Latin languages, adjectives must agree in number and gender with the nouns they modify.

Fonds d'Artichauts Garnis
Crème Brûlée
Patatas Picantes
Cebollas Rellenas
Gnocchi Verdi
Pomodori Fritti
Chiles Rellenos
Frijoles Refritos

In many French recipe titles, however, the adjective is feminine (and singular) regardless of the gender of the noun because the words "à la mode" are implied, although frequently dropped. The adjective is therefore feminine to agree with the feminine word "mode."

Boeuf (à la mode) Bourguignonne
Poulet (à la mode) Niçoise
Ris de Veau (à la mode) Provençale
Oeufs (à la mode) Portugaise

But note that Italians seldom drop the "alla":

Ossobuco alla Milanese
Carciofi alla Romana

If English and French must be combined, don't try to make the adjective agree; use the masculine and singular form of the adjective.

Chicken Gratiné
Cherries Flambé
Beef Bourguignon

When the name of a dish is a dedication to a person, rather than "in the manner of" that person, the words "à la" are omitted, and there is no agreement of adjective and noun.

Oeufs Massena
Pêche Melba
Sole Carmen

ATTRIBUTION IN TITLES

Most food writers make use of recipes that are not their own invention. They can come from personal friends, from restaurants, from other published food writers, and from contributors, if the author is compiling a book of collected recipes. Whatever its source, such a recipe should be acknowledged, but doing so by means of the title—Mindy Horlick's Favorite Soup, Jack's Barbecue Sauce—is not the best way and should be used sparingly.

First, it can lead to index bloat, because the contributor's name must be indexed as well as the normal categories for the rest of the title (principal ingredient, kind of dish, or method of preparation). Second, unless the contributor is a celebrity, it gives the reader a sense of being shut out: Should I recognize the name "Mindy Horlick"? Who is "Jack"?

Attribution can be given in an acknowledgments section, or it can be given in the headnote. When the book is a collection, with many contributors, there will be a standard place for attribution. Usually the contributor's name is given in parentheses below the recipe title or at the end of the recipe.

If a recipe has been published elsewhere, the food writer must have permission in writing from the publisher (not the author), which will state exactly how the credit is to be phrased. In some cases a fee may be charged.

If the food writer wants to use names to lend authenticity to recipes, he should do so only occasionally and when the name might mean something to the reader (a celebrity, for example, or a famous chef). Rarely does this include his children or his wife or his next-door neighbor who helped to test the recipe. But if he does use unknown names, he should explain who Mindy Horlick and Jack are in the headnote and why the recipes are named for them.

SUBSIDIARY RECIPE TITLES

Many recipes are subsidiary to the main recipe—sauces, pastry crusts, garnishes, batters—and yet are complete recipes that can be used with other recipes as well. These subsidiary recipes should have distinctive titles of their own that are descriptive enough to be indexed, or used in cross-references, thus enabling the cook to find them easily.

POOR: Sauce
GOOD: Ricotta and Spinach Sauce

POOR: Frosting
GOOD: Vanilla Cream Frosting

POOR: Garnish
GOOD: Chocolate Leaves

When such a subsidiary recipe is used, the ingredients list for the main recipe should include a reference to it.

2 cups ricotta and spinach sauce (recipe follows)
Chocolate leaves (see below) for garnish

— *Headnotes* —

The headnote—a sentence or a paragraph commenting on the recipe that follows—can be a source of information, helping the reader to envision the dish, discussing ingredients, warning of any peculiarities, and giving alternative instructions. It can also be the spot the writer chooses to give attribution, or be just good reading. Not every recipe in a book or article needs a headnote; use them when you have something to say, even if only to recount an anecdote.

One of the masters of the art of headnote writing was Irma Rombauer, author of the original *Joy of Cooking*. Many of her headnotes have become classics, including this one for French-fried potatoes:

Konrad Bercovici tells the following story: Madame Schumann-Heink, the great opera singer, was sitting in front of an enormous steak. Caruso passed her table and seeing the huge portion of meat before the singer, he said: "Stina, you are not going to eat that alone!" "No," Schumann-Heink said, shaking her fine old head. "No, not alone. With potatoes." Two to one they were French-fried potatoes.

HELP THE READER ENVISION THE DISH

Suprêmes de Volaille en Goujons

Goujons are tiny fish, like whitebait, and when fillet of sole is cut into strips and fried for a garnish, it is called *en goujons;* thus it follows that anything cut into small slices can be described as *en goujons.*

Calzone

Calzone, which means trouser leg in Italian, is a pizza folded in half like a turnover.

Sliced Pasta Roll with Spinach Filling

In this dish an entire sheet of pasta dough is rolled up with stuffing, wrapped in cheesecloth, and boiled. When cool, it is sliced, seasoned with a béchamel and tomato sauce, and baked very briefly in a very hot oven. It is a delicious change of pace from all the familiar pasta dishes, and lends itself to a very attractive presentation.

TELL HOW TO SERVE IT

Leg of Lamb in a Spicy Yogurt Sauce

If you are having guests for dinner, this is quite impressive—a whole leg dressed with a rich sauce and garnished with almonds and golden raisins. I often serve it with sweet yellow rice and a green vegetable.

Confiture d'Oignons

A distinct product of the nouvelle cuisine, onion marmalade always elicits the pleasantest sounds of satisfaction and can be served in a variety of ways—in small croustades or on rounds of lightly toasted French bread as an hors d'oeuvre, or as a meat accompaniment.

Mexican Chicken Salad

I created this dish because of my passion for Mexican food. I usually serve it with a side dish of Green Bean Salad tossed in a creamy horseradish dressing, some warmed Buttermilk Corn Bread, and a chilled bottle of my favorite white wine.

DISCUSS INGREDIENTS

The headnote is a good place to explain an important ingredient, and to suggest substitutes for hard-to-find ingredients or to tell whether they are optional. Just as important, the writer can caution the reader not to attempt the dish if something essential is not available.

Sautéed Calf's Liver with Onions, Venetian Style

What you need for this dish is, above everything else, a butcher able and willing to slice calf's liver to an even thinness of ¼ inch. The thinner liver is, the faster it cooks, and the faster it cooks, the sweeter it tastes.

Kataifi

Kataifi pastry is like shredded wheat, but soft. Buy it at Near Eastern shops, or substitute shredded wheat.

Clams in Romescu Sauce

One of the sauce ingredients, aguardiente, is a powerful Spanish liqueur made from the pressings of grape skins. Although only one teaspoon is required, it adds a special spark to the sauce and should not be eliminated. Its Italian equivalent, grappa, is available in most liquor stores.

MUSHROOM PÂTÉ

If the addition of baking powder seems odd to you, it does make a lighter, more palatable finished dish.

DISCUSS METHODS OF PREPARATION

The headnote can be used to warn the cook of any peculiarities in the dish or any difficulties or tips in preparation, and to point up things to be done ahead.

STUFFED MEXICAN FLANK STEAK

The preparation of this dish will not be a study in efficiency even in the hands of the most experienced cooks. Small portions of the stuffing tend to fall out of the meat rolls. Nevertheless, it is a fine dish for winter dining.

OVEN-BROWNED TOMATOES

In this recipe, all the wateriness of fresh tomatoes is drawn off through long, slow cooking. Don't let the quantity of oil alarm you. Nearly all of it gets left behind in the pan.

PECAN CRISPS

These cookies must be made a day in advance.

FRIED STUFFED BABY SQUID

Although the squid may be stuffed in advance, the frying must be done at the very last moment. Do not try to use large squid—they are too thick and will toughen when fried in this manner.

SUKIYAKI

If the food processor is to be used to cut the beef into gossamer slices, you must partially freeze the beef so that it offers some resistance to the cutting blade and will stand up against the machine's force rather than being reduced to pulp.

GIVE ATTRIBUTION

RED PEPPER QUICHE

An unusual quiche from Word of Mouth, one of New York's finest caterers.

ARTICHOKE HEARTS WITH SHRIMP AND CURED HAM

El Amparo is one of Madrid's finest and most stylish new restaurants. A tasting menu gives a sampling of the best the chef has to offer, and on a recent visit I was particularly taken with these stuffed artichoke hearts.

PAIN D'ÉPICE

Lindsey Shere, who is in charge of pastries and desserts at Chez Panisse restaurant in Berkeley, contributed this truly wonderful French spice bread. Pain d'épice improves if it is aged for a few days.

—*Ingredients List*—

The ingredients list is the real clue to the reader whether the recipe is something he wants to try. A quick glance can reveal to the experienced cook whether the combination of flavors is appealing, and to the novice whether the ingredients are familiar and easily obtainable. To both, the list should serve as a shopping list.

Its most important function, however, is to state clearly what food is called for in the recipe and, briefly, the form it should be in.

Equipment, utensils, and special items such as kitchen parchment, string, etc., are not ingredients and should not be included in the listing. Most cooks will read through a recipe before starting to see what they will need, but if the writer wants to specify equipment, it should be done under a separate heading, either before the ingredients list or at the end of the recipe.

LIST INGREDIENTS IN ORDER OF USE

Listing ingredients in their order of use is one of the cardinal rules in modern recipe writing. It is inexcusable to force the cook to search through a haphazard listing of ingredients in order to find what is called for next in the instructions. A chronological listing also makes it easy for the author, editor, and proofreader to check instructions against ingredients to make sure that nothing has been left out.

The practice of placing the main ingredient at the top of the list, regardless of the order in which it is called for, is not recommended. Recipes on the backs of packages sometimes do this to highlight the company's product, but many companies are phasing out this practice, and there is no call for it in ordinary published recipes.

The listing order should follow the instructions literally. If they say, "Mince the onion and garlic," the ingredients list should list the onion first and the garlic second. If the instructions say, "Sauté the onion in the oil until wilted," the onion should be listed before the oil.

If the writer is calling for pastry dough, or a similar ingredient for which instructions are given elsewhere, it can be listed first with the cross-reference, "Pastry dough (page 333)"; the first sentence in the instructions then can be, "Prepare the pastry dough." Or it can be listed in order of use, assuming that the cook will read the list of ingredients first and recognize that this additional recipe must be prepared.

When an instruction says, "Add the remaining ingredients," it is a help to the cook if the remaining ingredients are in some kind of logical order in the ingredients list—herbs together, for instance, and seasonings together.

AVOID ABBREVIATIONS

In most cookbooks, space is not a problem and there is no reason to use any abbreviations in the ingredients list. They can be misread (T. and t., particularly, or even Tbsp. and tsp.) and make the page look choppy. Some magazines and newspapers, however, do use abbreviations because of space limitations, and the proper forms are these:

centigram	cg
centiliter	cl
deciliter	dl
dozen	doz.
gram	g or gm
kilogram	kg
liter	l
milligram	mg
milliliter	ml
ounce	oz.
pound	lb.
cup	c.
quart	qt.
tablespoon	Tbsp. or T.
teaspoon	tsp. or t.

The word "page" can be abbreviated if necessary.

1 cup crème fraîche (p. 333)

DESCRIBE THE INGREDIENTS AS THEY ARE PURCHASED OR MEASURED

The food writer should do the work for the cook and describe the ingredients called for in a way that will help in shopping. The quantity "3 cups sliced zucchini" may mean nothing to a novice shopper—at the supermarket, zucchini is sold by the pound or the piece. The author should weigh the zucchini and estimate how many pounds it will take to produce 3 cups sliced.

POOR: 3 cups sliced zucchini
GOOD: 1 pound zucchini, thinly sliced (about 3 cups)

POOR: 4 cups cooked pasta shells
GOOD: 8 ounces pasta shells, cooked

The author should also be aware of can sizes and the amounts they contain. Count the number of anchovies in a 2-ounce can (10 to 12) and take this into account when calling for a specified number of anchovies. Maybe 1 can would do just as well as 15 anchovies. A 28-ounce can of plum tomatoes contains 2 cups, drained. A 13¾-ounce can of chicken or beef broth contains 1¾ cups.

The following are suggested ways to list commonly used ingredients:

Bean Curd (Tofu): Specify "firm" or "soft" and list in ounces.

14 ounces firm bean curd (2 cakes)
6 to 8 ounces fresh soft bean curd

Butter: Butter is purchased by the pound, and it frequently comes in quarter-pound sticks, marked off in tablespoons, eight to the stick. Thus it is useful to list small amounts of butter by the tablespoon, but ¼ pound or more by pounds. It is also helpful to list the number of sticks in addition to pounds. The practice of listing butter by cups is not recommended. It is too cumbersome to measure butter in a cup and seems dated.

2 tablespoons butter
¼ pound (1 stick) butter
½ pound plus 4 tablespoons (2½ sticks) butter

Canned Foods: List by weight and, where appropriate, by cups. It is helpful to add cup measurements for those cooks who might have smaller or larger cans than the writer is recommending.

1 can (7 ounces) tuna fish
1 can (28 ounces) Italian plum tomatoes, about 2 cups drained

Cheese: List by weight, and also by cups if it is grated.

¼ pound Parmesan cheese, or 1 cup freshly grated
4 ounces Gruyère cheese, grated (1 cup)

Chocolate: List by weight and squares when appropriate.

1 ounce (1 square) unsweetened chocolate

Fish and Shellfish: List by weight, or by the piece with weight following. Shellfish is presumed to be raw, or uncooked, so it is not necessary to say so.

6 halibut steaks, about 4 ounces each
1½ pounds fresh tuna in one piece
1 whole striped bass (about 6 pounds, cleaned)
24 cherrystone clams on the half shell
½ pound crabmeat, fresh or canned
3 lobsters, about 1¼ pounds each
4 pounds small mussels, scrubbed and debearded
2 pounds medium shrimp, about 50

Flour: List by tablespoons and cups, not weight. Although it is more accurate to weigh flour rather than measure it, American cooks are not used to the practice and most established bakers (Bernard Clayton, Marion Cunningham, and Evan Jones) have abandoned it.

If you must call for that common flour measurement "⅞ cup," change it to "1 cup less 2 tablespoons."

Fruit: List by weight, or by the piece with a size description (small, medium, large). Where the amount of juice is important to the recipe, list by the piece and by the amount of juice needed.

1 medium lemon, about 3 tablespoons juice

Gelatin: List by envelopes and spoonfuls, not ounces. (For conversion, 1 envelope = ¼ ounce.)

1 envelope (1 scant tablespoon) unflavored gelatin

Meat and Poultry: List by weight, or by the piece with weight or size following.

1 pound veal scallops (8 pieces), pounded paper thin
1 whole lamb breast (about 2 pounds), boned
4 loin lamb chops, each about 1 inch thick
1 duck (4½ to 5 pounds), cut into quarters
6 ready-to-cook quail, about 1¼ pounds total weight

2 pounds skinned and boned chicken breasts
or
6 skinless and boneless chicken breast halves

Nuts: If whole, list by weight (and cups, if desired). If chopped, list by cups.

Sugar: List by tablespoons or cups, not weight.

Vegetables: List by weight, or by the piece with weight following. Exceptions are onions, shallots, scallions, and bell peppers that are to be chopped and used for flavoring. These can be listed by piece only, or by volume when chopped. Give sizes for cans and packages of frozen vegetables.

1 fennel bulb, about 1 pound
¼ pound fresh snow peas, or 1 package (6 ounces) frozen
6 to 8 carrots, grated (about 3 cups)
1 package (10 ounces) frozen spinach
½ cup chopped onion
1 can (28 ounces) Italian plum tomatoes
1 tablespoon grated fresh ginger

Water: Because water does not have to be purchased, it is always omitted from the ingredients list when general amounts are called for, such as for boiling pasta, for covering a vegetable or another ingredient with water and then bringing to a boil, for adding to a pan to surround custards, etc.

There is disagreement, however, about listing water when the amount is essential to the dish, when the water must be at a specific temperature, and when something must be dissolved in it and thus it becomes a part of the final dish. We recommend that such specific amounts of water be listed so that the cook will know to measure it and have it ready when called for in the instructions.

Yeast: For active dry yeast, list by envelope and spoonfuls. For cake yeast, list by weight. Active dry yeast comes in sealed envelopes holding 1 tablespoonful, as well as in 4-ounce jars and in bulk in health food stores; cake yeast comes in ½-ounce and 2-ounce sizes.

GIVE ALTERNATIVES WHEN APPROPRIATE

When something very specific and unfamiliar is called for, or when the ingredient is expensive and difficult to find, it is helpful to know that something else can be used.

½ pound mostaccioli or other tubular pasta
4 Chinese sausages, diced, or ½ cup diced cooked ham
4 juniper berries, or 1 tablespoon gin
5 squab, or, more economically, 4 Cornish game hens

INCLUDE ONLY SHORT INSTRUCTIONS

Knowing the audience for a recipe is especially important here. Experienced cooks like to have the ingredients list tell them almost everything, so they can assemble all the prepared ingredients beforehand—not one at a time, as in the instructions.

But if the recipes are to appeal to a wide audience, the writer should include only simple instructions. Long, complicated instructions look out of place in the ingredients list and intimidate some readers.

POOR: 2 strips lemon peel, cut ½ inch wide, 2½ inches long, and then into julienne strips
4 ounces lean salt pork, diced into ⅜-inch pieces and blanched (boiled 5 minutes in 2 quarts of water, and drained)
3 medium-size leeks, white part only, washed, quartered lengthwise, chopped in ½-inch pieces (2½ cups)

GOOD: 2 eggs, separated
1 cup lentils, washed and drained
4 slices white bread, crusts removed
1 large acorn squash, halved lengthwise

It is helpful, however, to warn the cook that ingredients should be at room temperature, thawed, or soaked—preparations that should be done ahead. It is frustrating for the cook to start assembling a dish only to find that there are chores that should have been performed hours earlier.

> 1 package (10 ounces) frozen corn kernels, thawed
> 4 hard-boiled eggs
> 3 tablespoons butter, at room temperature
> 2 cups dried lima beans, soaked overnight in cold water
> Prebaked 9-inch pie shell (page 333)
> 1 ounce dried boletus mushrooms, soaked in warm water for 30 minutes

Be sure the preparation appears in the proper place, which is not necessarily after the comma.

> ¼ cup parsley, chopped fine

This means that the cook must collect ¼ cup of parsley sprigs and then chop them. What is usually meant, however, is that the ingredient must be chopped before it is measured.

> ¼ cup finely chopped parsley

Similarly, "2 cups canned tomatoes, drained" means that the cook must measure 2 cups with their juice and then drain them, a not very practical way to proceed. What is usually meant is "2 cups drained canned tomatoes."

There is a quantitative difference, however, between such ingredients as the following:

> 1 cup pecans, coarsely chopped
> 1 cup coarsely chopped pecans

Instead of automatically changing for the sake of consistency, the editor should query the author as to which amount is called for.

If melted butter is called for, give the measurement and follow it with the word "melted." Otherwise an inexperienced cook may melt a large amount of butter and measure out the amount called for, although the two are the same in the following example.

POOR: 4 tablespoons melted butter
GOOD: 4 tablespoons butter, melted

The same rule should apply to whipped cream, because 6 tablespoons of cream, whipped, will give a volume greater than 6 tablespoons of whipped cream.

POOR: 6 tablespoons whipped cream
GOOD: 6 tablespoons heavy cream, whipped

GIVE EQUIVALENTS WHEN APPROPRIATE

Many measurements are approximate, but it is helpful to the cook to know about how much he should have after chopping, slicing, grating, etc. And although it is preferable to list the ingredient in the manner in which it is purchased, in some cases the exact measurement is important to the dish and should be listed first.

½ pound mushrooms, sliced (2 cups)
1 large sweet red pepper, seeded and diced (1 cup)
1 bunch celery (enough to make 4 cups sliced)
Grated peel of 2 small lemons (2 tablespoons)
1¼ cups egg whites (about 8)
4 cups corn kernels, cut from 6 to 8 ears

BE SPECIFIC

It can be frustrating to the cook if he isn't sure what the recipe calls for. The writer should be specific, and then use the same terminology throughout—don't call for dry mustard in one recipe and powdered mustard in another. This is an area where an alert editor should spot inconsistencies.

Bouquet Garni: Tell what herbs to use in parentheses.

Bouquet garni (fresh parsley, bay leaf, dried thyme)

Bread Crumbs: Fresh or dried? Coarse or fine?

Butter: Call just for butter, or specify unsalted butter each time. The term "unsalted" is preferable to "sweet" because that is usually the way it is labeled.

Canned Foods: Are they drained? And do you save the liquid?

Chicken Breasts: Specify whole or half breasts, boned or with bone in.

Cloves: Whole or ground?

Couscous: Quick-cooking or regular?

Cream: Heavy or light?

Eggs: Eggs are presumed to be large unless otherwise specified.

Endive: Curly (also called *frisée*) or Belgian?

Flour: Flour is presumed to be all-purpose unless otherwise specified. But there are many other flours readily available—rye, whole wheat, semolina, self-rising, instant—and if the author uses these frequently it would be best to specify all-purpose flour when that is called for.

Because today's flour does not have to be sifted for the majority of recipes, it is not necessary to specify sifted or unsifted. But when sifted flour is important to the recipe, include the sifting in the instructions.

Gelatin: Unflavored?

Ginger: Fresh or powdered?

Herbs: Fresh or dried? If fresh, give the dried equivalents when appropriate, usually 3 to 1. Note that dill and chives are snipped; other herbs are chopped or minced.

Marsala and Sherry: Sweet or dry?

Mustard: Dry or prepared?

Nuts: Whole or shelled?

Peppers: Choose "bell" or "sweet" pepper and stick to it. Specify fresh or dried chili peppers and give type (Anaheim, jalapeño, etc.) or general description (small hot dried red chili).

Rice: Rice is presumed to be raw and long-grain unless otherwise specified.

Salt and Pepper: Give amounts if possible. Otherwise just call for "Salt and pepper." Do not say "to taste" in the ingredients list; it is neither a measurement nor a preparation. Put that in the instructions. Add the adjective "black" to pepper only if there could be confusion, as when white pepper or cayenne (ground red pepper) is also in the list.

Sesame Oil: The seasoning oil used in Asian cooking or the flavorless cooking oil?

Shortening: Specify butter, margarine, vegetable shortening, or lard. Shortening can also refer to oils used in baking.

Spices: Ground or whole? Nutmeg is usually grated.

Sugar: Sugar is presumed to be granulated unless otherwise specified. If two kinds of sugar are used in one recipe, list one as granulated and the other as confectioners' or brown. And in some recipes, the writer will want to specify superfine sugar.

Vinegar: Cider, white wine, red wine, distilled white, balsamic, raspberry, or other flavored vinegars?

Yeast: Active dry or cake?

Yogurt: Plain? Nonfat or low-fat?

BRAND NAMES AND TRADEMARKS

If the author has favorite brands of canned or packaged foods, he can discuss them in a separate section of the book or article, or in a note following the recipe. If they are used frequently in the ingredients list, it will look as if he is on the company payroll.

POOR: Crisco
GOOD: Solid vegetable shortening

POOR: Fleischmann's RapidRise yeast
GOOD: Fast-rising yeast

If, however, a particular brand is considered important, use it. It can sometimes be more confusing to the reader to try to figure out a euphemism for the brand name than if he is told outright. Tabasco is one of the few registered trademarks that are used routinely in recipes because there is no generic term for it; "hot pepper sauce" could mean many Asian products.

COMBINE DIFFERENT QUANTITIES OF THE SAME INGREDIENT

When the recipe calls for, say, 3 tablespoons of sugar at one stage of preparation and ½ cup at another stage, the entry in the ingredients list should give the total amount, with the larger amount first:

½ cup plus 3 tablespoons sugar

There is nothing more annoying than setting aside the flour, butter, or sugar called for in an ingredients list, only to find further along that more of the same is needed. This is particularly true of chopped ingredients, such as garlic, scallions, ginger; it is easier to do all the chopping at once. So combine the total quantity and use the instructions to tell how it is divided.

½ plus ⅓ cup flour
6 tablespoons olive oil
¼ cup snipped chives plus additional for garnish

Note a special rule for butter: Melted butter can be listed on a separate line from regular butter.

2 tablespoons butter
½ pound butter, melted

The word "divided" after a combined ingredient, such as "1 cup sugar, divided," adds nothing to the information. The cook will still have to read the instructions to find out how it is to be divided.

In a recipe with many ingredients, some of which are used in different quantities in several steps, it is preferable to use subheadings in the ingredients list to separate different elements in the recipe (see page 28). The ingredient can then be repeated in each element. This is particularly helpful with Asian recipes; soy sauce, ginger, and garlic, for example, are used in varying amounts in the seasoning sauce and the final assembly. Combining the total quantity of such ingredients would be confusing, and would diminish efficiency in organizing the ingredients before cooking.

DO NOT COMBINE DIFFERENT INGREDIENTS

Avoid combining ingredients on one line, unless space is extremely tight, because the eye can skip over one of them.

POOR: ½ cup each sugar, red wine vinegar, and apple jelly
GOOD: ½ cup sugar
½ cup red wine vinegar
½ cup apple jelly

Where this poor construction is unavoidable (in pamphlets or newspapers), supply emphasis by setting the word "each" in boldface or in italics. This will caution the cook to pay particular attention.

(See also page 38 about combining ingredients in instructions.)

REFERRING TO OTHER RECIPES

When calling for a preparation given elsewhere in the book, specify the quantity needed. "Recipe" is not a specific quantity. Specifying "1 cup" is not only clearer but allows the cook to use his own version of what is called for. (For the proper form in cross-references, see page 159.)

POOR: 1 recipe crème fraîche (page 333)
GOOD: 1 cup crème fraîche (page 333)

POOR: Piecrust (recipe follows)
GOOD: Double crust for a 9-inch pie (recipe follows)

The author should avoid unnecessary cross-references. It is intimidating, uses up valuable time, and involves the cook in much awkward page turning. In the following example, a béchamel has so few ingredients it is better to include them in the ingredients list and tell how to make the sauce in the instructions.

POOR: Béchamel sauce (page 333), omitting the nutmeg
GOOD: 2 tablespoons butter
2 tablespoons flour
1 cup milk
Salt and freshly ground pepper

OPTIONAL INGREDIENTS

Use the word "optional" after an ingredient only when it can be omitted without harm to the dish. This might be because something is expensive, hard to find, or not to everyone's liking, such as liqueurs.

Don't, however, overuse the word. Parsley in most dishes is optional and this doesn't need to be said. Garnishes are, in most cases, optional. Things like ice cream and whipped cream that would be nice accompaniments but are not integral to the dish can be suggested in the headnote or listed as optional in the ingredients list.

INEXACT AMOUNTS

Unspecified amounts of ingredients such as the following should be included in recipes for beginning cooks. If the audience is more sophisticated, or if there are space limitations, they may be omitted. Whatever the choice, they should be handled consistently.

Flour for dredging
Additional flour for rolling out dough or pastry
Butter or vegetable oil for oiling a pan
Lemon juice for acidulated water

There are several ways to word an ingredient when you might need more or less. All the following are acceptable.

2½ cups flour plus additional as needed
5 cups chicken stock (approximately)
½ cup sugar (more or less depending on the sweetness of the pears)
2 teaspoons ground cinnamon, or to taste

SUBHEADINGS WITHIN LIST

If a recipe has two or more distinct parts, list the ingredients for each part under its own subheading. (Keep the instructions together for the entire recipe; do not run them in between subheadings. But it is helpful for the reader to start a step corresponding to the subhead "To make the piecrust," for example.)

The piecrust:
The filling:

The Mexican beef:
The corn cakes:

When space limitations make subheadings an impossibility, a centered dash, or rule, may be set on a line by itself between groupings:

2 cups flour
1½ teaspoons baking soda
1 teaspoon baking powder
1 teaspoon vanilla powder

———

1 cup sour cream
8 tablespoons (1 stick) butter, melted
1 cup sugar
2 eggs

Many publications separate groups of ingredients with lines of space, but it isn't always clear that the ingredients that follow the spacing are not part of the previous grouping. If there are ingredients that do not fit logically under a heading, devise a word for them. "Assembly" and "glaze" are good in the following examples:

The chicken and marinade:
The seasoning sauce:
The assembly:

The pastry:
The filling:
The glaze:

—Instructions—

There are many proponents of the theory that a recipe can never be too explicit, and probably an equal number who prefer to make the instructions as short as possible, trusting the intelligence of the cook to know what is meant.

We propose a middle-of-the-road course leaning toward the explicit, which says that clarity and consistency are the two most important principles in writing instructions. This section deals with some of the specific ways to achieve these goals. Chapter 2, "The Language of Recipes," elaborates on the nuances.

The author must continually ask himself whether an inexperienced cook would need guidance, and if so, give it in language that is as clear as possible. Some food writers are notable for the feeling they create of being a wise, experienced, and comforting presence in the kitchen, anticipating questions and giving reassurances. One of these writers is Maida Heatter, whose recipes are exemplary for this quality. One of the least helpful, although at the same time a well-loved cookbook author, is Irma Rombauer (*Joy of Cooking*), who is often guilty of such statements as "Cook until done."

Compare their baking instructions for macaroons:

Joy of Cooking

Bake the macaroons in a slow oven (300 degrees) for about 25 minutes. Place the paper on a moist cloth. Remove the macaroons.

Maida Heatter's Book of Great Chocolate Desserts

Bake [the macaroons] for about 20 minutes, reversing the sheets top to bottom and front to back once to insure even baking. When done, the macaroons should be dry (but slightly soft) on the outside, moist and soft in the center. They will harden somewhat as they cool—don't overbake them.

Slide the papers off the cookie sheets. Let stand for about half a minute. Now the macaroons will be stuck to the paper. To remove them in the best classic manner, lift each piece of paper by holding two sides of it, and gently turn it upside down onto a work table or counter top. Brush the paper with water, using a pastry brush or wet cloth. Let it stand briefly. As you see the paper dry out over the cookies, wet it a second time. Let stand for a few minutes until the paper can be lifted off easily without tearing the bottom of the macaroons. If necessary, wet the papers a third time. Place the cookies right side up on racks to cool.

DIVIDE THE STEPS LOGICALLY

This is one of many instances when the food writer must do some of the work for the cook and guide him through the recipe.

As the writer tests the recipe, he should keep track of what is done and in what order. Then, while retesting, he should divide the procedures logically. The first step should include preliminary preparation—preheating the oven, buttering a pan, bringing water to a boil, heating oil for deep frying; the final step should contain finishing instructions—tossing with a sauce, glazing under the broiler, topping with whipped cream, garnishing with parsley. In between, each ingredient and preparation should be dealt with in logical progression—first this and then that—with no more than five or six lines to each step.

NUMBERED VS. UNNUMBERED STEPS

The advantages to numbered steps are both psychological and practical. Psychologically, the numbered steps give an impression of orderliness to the recipe, imparting a subliminal message that the recipe is less daunting than it might otherwise appear. On a more practical level, the numbers enable the cook to keep track of where he is in the preparation. Moreover, they can be used to key variations to a master recipe, as in the example below.

> *Variation:* For molded risotto, prepare the risotto with Parmesan cheese through step 4. Lightly butter a 6-cup ring mold . . .

Some writers prefer paragraphed steps without numbers, which gives a more narrative look to the recipe. In this case, each new paragraph should be indented, and ideally, ample space should be left between paragraphs. Solid blocks of type are not easy to follow.

NO SURPRISES

Tell the reader immediately what needs to be done first, rather than referring to it later in the instructions.

> Preheat the oven to 350 degrees.
> *(Not later: Bake in a preheated 350-degree oven.)*
>
> Bring water to a boil for the pasta.
> *(Not later: Cook pasta in rapidly boiling water.)*
>
> Butter 12 muffin cups.
> *(Not later: Spoon the batter into 12 greased muffin cups.)*

Drain the tomatoes and reserve the juice.
(Not later: Add the juice from the tomatoes [when the ingredients list called just for canned tomatoes, drained].)

Cover a baking sheet with aluminum foil.
(Not later: Shape the macaroons on a foil-covered baking sheet.)

Arrange an oven rack in the highest position and preheat the oven to 450 degrees.
(Not later: Bake in the upper third of the preheated oven.)

Bring a kettle of water to the boil.
(Not later: Pour hot water into the pan to come halfway up the sides of the pudding.)

WHEN TO PREHEAT THE OVEN

Be very careful to give preheating instructions at the proper time, which is not automatically in the first step of the recipe. Too often, the following appears, showing careless writing of the recipe and an inattentive copy editor. There's that oven heating for the hour that the prunes are soaking.

1. Preheat the oven to 375 degrees. Generously butter a shallow baking dish.

2. Soak the prunes in the brandy for at least 1 hour, preferably longer.

The time required for preheating has given rise to heated discussion. Traditionalists insist that it takes 20 minutes for an oven to become thoroughly and evenly heated to the desired temperature for the baking of cakes and other delicate batters. Testing in the Rodale kitchens showed that modern gas and electric stoves heated to a uniform 350 degrees in about 8 minutes.

Meantime, during the energy crisis of the early 1980s, the United States Department of Agriculture employed a panel of trained testers who decided that the differences between the results of cold-oven and preheated versions of the same recipes were negligible and recommended that preheating be dispensed with.

The argument on the other side, however, is that cold foods put into a cold oven take longer to cook, and therefore use even more energy than does preheating the oven.

One way to cut down on cooking time for certain dishes is to bring them to a boil on the top of the stove before putting them in the oven. This is a trick used in restaurants and by many of the authors of articles and books on quick cooking.

BROILING AND GRILLING INSTRUCTIONS

Allow about 5 minutes to preheat a broiler, and 20 to 30 minutes to get charcoal to the white-ash stage. A gas grill turned to "high" will be hot in about 5 minutes.

Do not ask the cook to broil the food 12 inches from the source of heat, since most standard gas ovens have about 6 inches of space. If this is necessary to the outcome of the dish, use the headnote to warn the cook.

And not everyone has a professional range with a salamander, used for glazing a dish. It is not always as easy to glaze a dish in a broiler as it is in a salamander, so the writer should test it once in a regular broiler.

REFER TO EACH INGREDIENT AS IT IS USED

There are better ways to save space than to lump several ingredients in an instruction. It is confusing and can cause the cook to spend unnecessary time figuring out what is meant.

POOR: Add the next six ingredients.
GOOD: Add the carrots, onions, peppers, celery, parsley, and olives.

POOR: Combine the first five ingredients.
GOOD: Combine the tomatoes, onion, chilies, cilantro, and lime juice.

POOR: Put the dry ingredients in one bowl.
GOOD: Put the flour, salt, and baking powder in one bowl.

(See also pages 25 and 26 about combining ingredients in the ingredients list.)

DESCRIBE THE FOOD AT DIFFERENT STAGES

Give amounts if they were not indicated in the ingredients list.

> Cut the fennel into 1-inch dice; you should have about 3 cups.
>
> Open and drain the clams and reserve both clams and their juice. Chop the clams. There should be about 1 cup of clams and 1½ cups of juice.

Give a visual image when appropriate.

> Cut together the flour mixture, almonds, butter, and shortening until crumbled to the size of peas.
>
> Cut the mozzarella into finger-size sticks.
>
> Chop the garlic into pieces about the size of match-heads.
>
> The eggplant will look like a deflated, wrinkled balloon.

When appropriate and helpful, state the time it takes to complete a step and what the food should look or feel like.

> Beat the eggs with the sugar until they are thick and hold a mound that slowly sinks back into the mixture. It takes me about 10 minutes to do this with my electric hand mixer.
>
> When the mixture is set, the frittata will slide in the pan but the top will be liquid.
>
> As the sauce comes near the boil it will get lumpy—beat vigorously to smooth it out. It will be very thick.

Be clear about how to tell when a dish is done.

> Add the olives and continue cooking for another 10 minutes over low heat, or until the chops are tender when tested near the bone with the point of a small sharp knife.
>
> Continue baking for 10 minutes, or until the clams open.
>
> When finished, the onions should be brown and shiny and coated with the sauce.
>
> Bake the pie until nearly set, 40 to 45 minutes (the filling will still be somewhat wobbly in the center).

SHARE COOKING KNOWLEDGE

It is often helpful to know the reason for a procedure.

> Drain the bamboo shoots, drop the pieces into boiling water, and simmer about 5 minutes. This will remove the canned flavor.
>
> Spread the rock salt on the bottom of the pans. (The salt serves to keep the oysters from tipping and to retain heat.)
>
> Cut off any bone or stringy tendons from the veal, but don't remove every bit of gristle and fat; they add flavor and thicken the broth.
>
> Cook the rice for 18 minutes without stirring again. (Stirring releases starch, which makes the rice sticky.)
>
> Freeze this layer before adding the next or the colors will mix.
>
> Whisk the egg yolks to break them up, but don't make them foam or you will not be able to see when the custard is properly cooked.

> Beat the egg yolk and cream with a fork and brush it on the tops of the puffs only. If the glaze drips onto the baking sheet, it will glue the puff down and keep it from rising.

The phrase "if you wish" can often be annoying to a cook unless he is told why he might wish.

POOR: If you wish, you may arrange the coated pieces on a rack to dry for a brief period.

GOOD: If you have time, arrange the coated pieces on a rack to dry for a brief period. This will help the coating adhere.

REFERRING TO OPTIONAL INGREDIENTS

When an ingredient is entered in the ingredients list as optional, the instructions can refer to the ingredient as optional or not, as the writer and editor choose. For beginning cooks, it is perhaps best to do so.

INGREDIENTS LIST: ¼ cup grated Gruyère cheese, optional

INSTRUCTIONS: Gently stir in one third of the whites, then fold in half the remaining whites, half the broccoli, and 2 tablespoons of the cheese, if using.

INGREDIENTS LIST: Pinch of nutmeg, optional

INSTRUCTIONS: Season with salt, pepper, and optional nutmeg.

ALTERNATIVE INGREDIENTS

When an alternative is given in the ingredients list, it is not necessary to refer to it in the instructions unless there is a different procedure for the alternative.

UNNECESSARY

INGREDIENTS LIST:	2 cups coarsely chopped hazelnuts or walnuts
INSTRUCTIONS:	Add the lemon juice, orange rind, and hazelnuts.
INGREDIENTS LIST:	2 tablespoons butter or margarine
INSTRUCTIONS:	Heat the butter until melted.

NECESSARY

INGREDIENTS LIST:	¼ vanilla bean, or ½ teaspoon vanilla extract
INSTRUCTIONS:	1. Put the milk and split vanilla bean, if using, in a saucepan . . . 4. If using vanilla extract, add it at this point.
INGREDIENTS LIST:	¼ cup water or milk
INSTRUCTIONS:	Thoroughly blend the flour and vegetables, then stir in the water. If you want to use milk, add it at the end of the cooking—it will curdle if you add it now.
INGREDIENTS LIST:	½ pound fresh tomatillos, or 1 (13-ounce) can
INSTRUCTIONS:	If using fresh tomatillos, remove and discard the paperlike skins. Place the tomatillos in a saucepan with water to cover, bring to a boil, and cook 1 minute. Drain, then place them in a bowl of ice water. If using canned tomatillos, simply drain them in a strainer, rinse, and set aside.

AVOID REDUNDANCY

If the ingredient has an instruction attached to it in the ingredients list, it is not necessary to repeat the instruction in the steps.

POOR	GOOD
2 tablespoons salad oil ½ cup chopped onion 1 garlic clove, minced	2 tablespoons salad oil ½ cup chopped onion 1 garlic clove, minced
1. Heat the oil in a skillet and add the chopped onion and minced garlic.	1. Heat the oil in a skillet and add the onion and garlic.

POOR	GOOD
10 large potatoes, cooked and cooled	10 large potatoes, cooked and cooled
1. Cook the potatoes, cool, and cut into ½-inch cubes.	1. Peel the potatoes and cut into ½-inch cubes.

When referring to a mixture, identify it by the principal ingredient, not all its components, which is redundant and can create awkward hyphenation.

POOR: Pour in the remaining tomato juice–butter mixture.
GOOD: Pour in the remaining tomato juice mixture.

POOR: Blend in the onion-nut-raisin mixture.
GOOD: Blend in the onion mixture.

COMBINED INGREDIENTS

When an ingredient is a combined one, to be divided between two or more steps, use the words "of the" in the instructions, indicating that at that stage you are using part of the whole. It is also extremely helpful to tell the cook how much is remaining.

INGREDIENTS LIST: 2 cups sugar

INSTRUCTIONS: 1. Add 1½ cups of the sugar . . .
4. Add the remaining ½ cup sugar . . .

INGREDIENTS LIST: ¼ cup flour

INSTRUCTIONS: 2. Stir in 3 tablespoons of the flour.
3. Mix in the remaining 1 tablespoon flour.

When different amounts are used in a combined ingredient, use the word "the" in the instructions.

INGREDIENTS LIST: ½ cup plus 2 tablespoons flour

INSTRUCTIONS: 2. Whisk in the ½ cup flour.
4. Add the 2 tablespoons flour.

DESCRIBE SOME PROCEDURES UNIFORMLY

It is helpful to the cook if the writer uses uniform wording for identical procedures. Once having established the preferred wording, the writer should keep a file or list of such terms. The copy editor can be asked to follow through.

This type of formula writing (in moderation) has much to recommend it; the writer will not have to grope for fresh wording each time and can be confident that nothing has been left out (assuming the original wording was carefully chosen). The cook is given complete information in each recipe. Some examples follow:

> Heat the oil until the first tiny bubbles form and a few small wisps of smoke appear.
>
> Roll the dough on a floured surface to a thickness of ⅛ inch.
>
> Heat a wok over high heat until a bead of water evaporates on contact.
>
> Warm the egg whites slightly over hot water or swirl over a gas flame until barely warm. Add the cream of tartar and beat them until they stand in soft peaks.

UTENSILS

Describe the pan when appropriate.

> Bring the wine, sugar, and vanilla to a simmer in a large saucepan (a big oval Dutch oven is ideal).
>
> Choose a skillet that can later accommodate all the liver in a single layer without crowding.
>
> The deeper your soufflé dish the taller your basket can be. I used a 2½-quart soufflé dish, 7 inches in diameter and 4 inches high.
>
> In a good-sized skillet (the broader the skillet the faster the sauce will thicken), slowly sauté the onion . . .
>
> Lightly brush a 9-inch cake or pie pan with melted butter (a Pyrex pan lets you see how the bottom layer is browning).

Many times the utensil is implied and a description is unnecessary, unless the recipe is for beginning cooks. The words in parentheses may be omitted.

> Whisk together (in a bowl) the salt, pepper, vinegar, and oil.
>
> Scoop out the pulp into a (medium-size) bowl, leaving ½-inch shells.
>
> (Using a pastry brush), brush the baking dish with melted butter.

When possible, use the same pan, bowl, colander, or food processor container for several different steps so that the cook has not used every piece of equipment in the kitchen.

> Wipe the saucepan clean and pour the strained sauce back into it.

Avoid Exact Pan Sizes

Do not give exact pan sizes unless it is important to the outcome of the recipe. It can be unnerving to the inexperienced cook with only a few pans to choose from.

POOR: Sauté the onions in a 10-inch skillet.
GOOD: Sauté the onions in a medium-size skillet.

POOR: Heat ¼ cup of the oil in a 12-inch skillet and sauté the mushrooms.
GOOD: Heat ¼ cup of the oil in a wide skillet and sauté the mushrooms. The pan must be large enough so that the mushrooms aren't crowded, which will make them steam rather than brown.

POOR: Tie the veal tightly, place in a casserole, and pour the marinade over.
GOOD: Tie the veal tightly, place in a deep-sided casserole just large enough to hold it snugly, and pour the marinade over. (If the casserole is too big, the sauce will burn.)

Avoid Monotony in Specifying Utensils

Starting every sentence with the utensil is boring to read, and in some cases it sounds as if English is not the author's native language.

POOR: In a heavy-bottomed casserole, melt the butter.
GOOD: Melt the butter in a heavy-bottomed casserole.

POOR: In a large covered saucepan fitted with a collapsible vegetable steamer, bring 1 inch of water to a boil.
GOOD: Put a collapsible vegetable steamer in a large saucepan, add 1 inch of water, cover, and bring to a boil.

POOR: In an 8-inch frying pan, over a medium flame, combine butter and oil and heat for a minute or two.
GOOD: Combine butter and oil in a small frying pan and heat over a medium flame for a minute or two.

TELL HOW TO KEEP SOMETHING WARM

The instruction "keep warm" can be frustrating to an inexperienced cook. Tell the reader how to go about this.

> If you are not ready to serve, unmold the cabbage and finish the sauce. Turn a bowl upside down over the platter with the cabbage and sauce and set in a 200-degree oven. It will keep for a good half hour.
>
> Keep warm in the turned-off oven with the door ajar.
>
> Set the cover askew and keep warm over barely simmering water.
>
> Cover the chicken loosely with foil while preparing the sauce. (If covered too closely, the chicken will steam from retained heat.)

A FINAL CHECK FOR THE AUTHOR AND EDITOR

Be sure to instruct the cook to remove something inedible before the dish is to be served. This could be a bouquet garni, a cinnamon stick, or a bay leaf.

—*Notes*—

A note comes at the end of a recipe and is a useful repository for supplemental information that would be awkward in the recipe itself. It can be used to discuss ingredients and preparation or to suggest accompaniments. Confine the information in a note to only one or two of these aspects.

Because a headnote and a note can serve some of the same functions, be consistent about where the information is placed. Do not discuss ingredients or preparation or accompaniments in the headnote in one place and in a note at the end of a recipe in another.

Notes are also easily cross-referenced. This is particularly useful when a note is used to elaborate on an instruction (see below).

GIVE SHORT INSTRUCTIONS

When an ingredient carries an instruction that might need elaboration, this can often be done best in a note.

½ cup buttered fresh bread crumbs (see note)

Note: To make buttered crumbs, melt 2 tablespoons butter in a small pan. Tear 2 slices of bread, without crusts, into very small pieces. Remove the pan from the heat and toss the bread with the melted butter.

½ pound blanched salt pork (see note)

Note: To blanch the salt pork, cover with boiling water and let stand for 5 minutes. Drain.

½ cup lamb or chicken broth (see note)

Note: To make lamb broth, do not use the lamb bones as indicated. That is to say, do not scatter them around the lamb as it roasts. Put the uncooked lamb bones in a small kettle with water to cover and add salt and pepper. Add a small peeled onion, 1 bay leaf, and ½ cup chopped carrot. Simmer about 45 minutes and strain.

GIVE ALTERNATIVE INSTRUCTIONS

The note is a handy place to suggest other ways to prepare or cook the dish, information that would be cumbersome in the recipe itself.

Note: All recipes given here for the grill can also be executed in a broiler, placing the fish 4 inches away from the heat element.

Note: To make this pastry in a food processor, combine dry ingredients with butter and solid shortening in processor, pulsing briefly until crumbly. Do not over-mix. Transfer to a mixing bowl and proceed to add sour cream and liquid by hand, as in step 2.

Note: If you want to make this soup in a pressure cooker, sauté the leeks and onions uncovered, blend in the flour, cook it, and blend in the liquid, salt, and potatoes as described. Cover the pan, bring rapidly to full pressure, and cook exactly 5 minutes. Release pressure at once. Simmer for 5 minutes or so to develop its taste, then complete the soup as described.

Note: I tried this in the microwave oven, and although the fat rendered nicely, the skin turned tougher than leather.

GIVE INSTRUCTIONS FOR STORING AND REHEATING

Note: If frozen, the casserole should be removed from the freezer and placed in the refrigerator overnight, defrosted at room temperature for 4 to 6 hours, and then baked at the oven temperature and for the baking time in the recipe. (If you don't have time to bring it to room temperature, place in a cold oven and double the baking time.)

Note: If you don't want to serve the trout right away, remove gently from the cooking liquid, drain, and wrap each separately in lightly oiled plastic—trout that cool together stick together.

Note: This may be cooked a day or two in advance. When cold, cover and refrigerate. To serve, reheat slowly, basting with sauce, then cover and keep at the barest simmer for 5 minutes. You may have to thin out the sauce with a little bouillon; retaste for seasoning.

EXPLAIN AN INGREDIENT

2 to 3 tablespoons raspberry vinegar (see note)

Note: Since raspberry vinegars vary in strength, use the lesser amount if yours seems particularly strong.

6 to 8 cups assorted bones and scraps (see note)

Note: Do not use lamb or pork bones unless you need a particularly strong-tasting broth.

½ cup finely chopped pork (see note)

Note: Two half-inch-thick pork chops, totaling about ½ pound, will give you this amount of meat. Chop it in a food processor.

1½ cups rich broth (see note)

Note: Use beef broth for beef croquettes; chicken for ham, veal, pork, and chicken; fish stock for seafood croquettes.

Prepared sausage casing (see note)

Note: The sausage casings we used in preparing this recipe were natural beef round casings, 40 to 43 millimeters. See page 333 for instructions on preparing them.

GIVE HELPFUL ADVICE OR TIPS

Note: In hot weather, it's advisable to refrigerate cakes iced with this frosting.

Note: Do not substitute margarine for butter in this recipe because it has slightly greater shortening power than butter, meaning that your shortbread is likely to run all over the baking sheet.

Note: In Italy we bring the pot to the table and serve the clams a few at a time so they don't get cold.

Note: If frozen peas are to be used, empty them frozen into a sieve and pour boiling water over them. Let drain. Further cooking is not necessary.

Note: Your mixer must be well adjusted so that the base of the whip scrapes lightly against the bottom of the bowl, or ½ to 1 inch of mixture at bottom will not mix evenly with the cream. To prevent this, slide a rubber spatula between the side of the bowl and the mixer blades—being careful not to let the spatula get caught in the blades.

SUGGEST ALTERNATIVE INGREDIENTS

1½ pounds smoked andouille (see note)

Note: To be genuinely authentic, smoked andouille, which is common in Louisiana, should be used. But kielbasa will produce a very satisfactory gumbo.

18 imported black olives (see note)

Note: Do not use California black olives for this dish; they are too bland. If imported black olives are not available, use pitted green olives.

TELL WHERE TO FIND AN INGREDIENT

1 tablespoon fish sauce (see note)

Note: Fish sauce, called nuoc mam or nam pla, is available in bottles in Asian groceries and supermarkets.

2 cups cornmeal, preferably imported (see note)

Note: Imported cornmeal (referred to as raw polenta) is widely available in specialty shops that offer imported foods and in grocery stores that specialize in Italian foods.

3 whole anchovies packed in salt (see note)

Note: Anchovies packed in salt are available in many specialty stores where imported Italian and Greek groceries are sold.

2 teaspoons garam masala (see note)

Note: Garam masala is a basic blend of Indian spices and varies from Indian cook to Indian cook. It is available in bottles and tins from specialty food shops.

TELL WHAT TO DO WITH LEFTOVERS

Note: If you have leftover eggplant slices, serve them folded into some lightly beaten plain yogurt. To reheat leftover pilaf, sauté it in hot oil with scallions and serve it as a light lunch.

Note: You will have ½ pound of frozen puff pastry left over from the vegetable pies. Freeze it, or use the pastry for a fruit tart. Thaw pastry and roll into two 8-inch rounds. . . .

Note: Leftover cooked strands of spaghetti squash are good cold in a salad dressed with a tangy vinaigrette.

Note: Leftover sauce from the chicken is excellent on pasta.

GIVE MENU AND SERVING SUGGESTIONS

Giving serving suggestions is always a helpful device, particularly for unusual dishes. If it is done frequently, however, a separate subheading, such as Menu Suggestions, may be more appropriate than a note.

Note: Spoon over rice pilaf (page 333) and accompany with Armenian cucumber and yogurt salad (page 333).

Note: Jellied consommé would make a nice first course. Serve the chicken with a purée of peas or green beans and watercress plus rice or homemade mashed potatoes.

SUGGEST AN APPROPRIATE WINE

Note: A light red wine, such as a Beaujolais or a California gamay, will complement this robust chowder.

Note: Chinese dishes are often best accompanied by good German wine—a Riesling, for instance.

— *Servings* —

When Alice B. Toklas submitted the recipes for her cookbook to a publisher, she was queried by an editor for the yields of each recipe. "How can I foretell how hungry my guests will be when they sit down to dine?" she is said to have replied.

And, indeed, the number of servings is a very personal matter, depending on the appetite of each diner. It also depends on how many courses are served at a meal. But if the writer sets a realistic standard and follows it, readers will learn very quickly whether his four servings are theirs.

Don't rely on home economists and others who have formulas for such things ("Allow ½ cup of vegetables per serving") because they're often not realistic. The size of a serving will vary with the simplicity or richness of the dish. The only way to determine a proper serving is to serve the dish several times to family and guests.

For most cookbooks, recipes should be planned for four to six servings. They can then be easily doubled for entertaining.

HOW TO WORD IT

Be careful in phrasing the yield. There is a subtle distinction between "serves" and "servings." We prefer the latter.

Serves 4: This implies that the amount is enough to feed any four persons the cook invites to dinner.

4 servings: This means that the recipe will produce four average portions. It does not mean that there is enough for seconds for four hearty eaters.

The servings are usually preceded by the word "yield" rather than "makes."

Yield: 4 servings

Some food writers prefer to give the yield by weight, measure, or other quantity, depending on the specialty of the recipes. This is frequently done with desserts.

Yield: 4 cups
Yield: 1 loaf, serving 8
Yield: One 11-inch tart
Yield: 3 dozen 2-inch cookies

WHERE TO PLACE IT

The yield can be placed either at the top of the recipe, under the title, or at the end, preferably on its own line. Whichever position is chosen, it should be done consistently so the cook knows where to look for it.

BE INFORMATIVE

It is helpful to give the cook further information when appropriate:

Yield: 1 cup, or enough for ¾ pound pasta
4 servings as an entrée, 6 as an appetizer
5 servings (10 patties)
4 servings (two 8-inch skewers per serving)
6 servings with other dishes in a Chinese meal
Enough to frost and fill a 9-inch two-layer cake
4 servings, with leftovers

— *Variations* —

Listing variations at the end of a recipe allows the writer to suggest ways to vary the dish, either in ingredients or preparation, but the variations should be more substantive than just omitting the mushrooms. Use them only when they are interesting and appropriate, not with every recipe.

> *Variation:* When the rice is done, at the end of step 1, swirl in 1 tablespoon of pesto. Omit the basil in step 2.
>
> *Variation:* For bran muffins, follow the directions for the blueberry muffins, substituting 1½ cups of All-Bran for the blueberries and decreasing the flour to 2½ cups.
>
> *Variation:* For a less expensive but equally tasty dish, replace the champagne with 1 bottle of still wine plus 1½ tablespoons balsamic vinegar.

If the variations should be included in the index, give them titles.

> *Variation*
>
> Potato and Celery Root Gratin: Substitute peeled celery root slices for one third the amount of potatoes, sandwiching the celery root between two layers of potatoes.

Variation

Asparagus or Broccoli Quiche: Substitute 1 to 1½ cups blanched or steamed asparagus or broccoli for the tomatoes and basil. Toss the vegetable quickly in a small amount of butter in a skillet over medium heat to dry it out and enhance the flavor, then scatter over the crust with the cheese and custard.

—2—

The Language of Recipes

THE LANGUAGE OF RECIPES in America is the English language, the same that is used by all literate American authors of fiction and non-fiction. The better one writes, the better one is able to communicate, and communication is the fundamental purpose of written recipes.

In Chapter 1 we pointed out the form in which recipes should appear and how the different elements should be used to make the author's intentions clear to readers. In this chapter we deal with some points of grammar and choice of words, because a recipe must meet the same standards of English as any other piece of explanatory prose in order to achieve the goals of accuracy and clarity.

We do not attempt to cover all aspects of good writing (about which there are many excellent books). There are, however, many expressions and subtleties that are peculiar to recipes, and those are what will concern us here.

—*Style and Substance*—

Once style has been established by the author and editor, it can be a temptation for the copy editor to change it to something possibly more felicitous. The mark of an experienced and careful copy editor is the restraint he exercises in this regard. Changing acceptable style to something arbitrarily preferred—unless it is clearly mandated by the house rules of a book publisher, a magazine, or a newspaper—often is less indicative of good judgment than it is of the Itchy Pencil Syndrome.

In the following examples, the author's choice is perfectly acceptable and not in need of change:

AUTHOR: 1 garlic clove, smashed and peeled
COPY EDITOR: 1 garlic clove, crushed and peeled

AUTHOR: Heat the oven to 350 degrees.
COPY EDITOR: Preheat the oven to 350 degrees.

AUTHOR: Bring the sauce to the boil.
COPY EDITOR: Bring the sauce to a boil.

AUTHOR: 1 tablespoon water for each egg
COPY EDITOR: 1 tablespoon water per egg

A useful procedure employed by many experienced copy editors is to postpone the decision on whether to change something: Put a self-stick flag or make a dot in the margin of the copy each time there is a stylistic matter that might be changed. Hold off on the decision until the entire work has been read through. This can often give a much different perspective from the original impulse, and a wiser head can prevail.

To sum up: If the copy has been prepared consistently in one of the acceptable forms, let the author's choice of words (and idiosyncrasies) stand. Only the need for accuracy and clarity should override the author's right to say things the way he wants to.

—Parts of Speech—

ARTICLES

"A," "an," and "the" are often viewed as unnecessary words in recipe writing, taking up valuable space. But they add to ease and clarity in reading and should be retained except when space is severely limited. Even then, there are better ways to save the small space taken up by articles (see "Unnecessary Words" in this chapter). Many respected food magazines with a tight, multicolumn format cling to the abbreviated style; the writing is terse in order to fit the available space. But there is no logic in applying this principle to the modern cookbook, where space is adjusted to copy and not the other way around. One editor who prefers recipes without articles said it was more telegraphic and made the recipes seem shorter and easier to prepare, but to most readers it is jarring and distracting.

POOR: Cut veal into thinnest possible strips. Heat butter in skillet.
GOOD: Cut the veal into the thinnest possible strips. Heat the butter in a skillet.

POOR: Using slotted spoon, transfer veal to saucepan.
GOOD: Using a slotted spoon, transfer the veal to a saucepan.

When a series of ingredients is used, one "the" is enough to introduce it.

Combine the coriander, cumin, and turmeric in a small cup.

VERBS

Start sentences with verbs when appropriate and choose the strongest verb that best describes the action called for.

POOR: Make tiny holes all over the pastry shell with a fork.
GOOD: Prick the pastry shell all over with a fork.

POOR: Cook the chicken pieces until lightly browned.
GOOD: Sauté the chicken pieces until lightly browned.

POOR: Chop the almonds and garlic in a blender.
GOOD: Pulverize the almonds and garlic in a blender.

POOR: Combine the pears and the flour.
GOOD: Toss the pears with the flour.

The verb does not have to be changed for variety—that leads only to strained writing and inconsistency. If the verb is "pour" for one liquid, it should be "pour" for the next, not "put," "spoon," or "funnel," or any other contrivance. It can lead the cook to believe that there is something different about this process from the last.

Use the word "add" only in the sense of adding to other ingredients. You cannot add something to a pan when there is nothing else there.

POOR: Add the oil to a skillet.
GOOD: Heat the oil in a skillet.

"Add" also is not the same as "stir in" or "combine."

> Add the vinegar and tomatoes, stirring to combine.
> Stir in the basil, pepper, and salt.
> Add the mixture to the grapes, tossing to combine.

Singular nouns connected by "or" take a singular verb.

> Water, potato water, or milk is the liquid commonly used in making yeast breads.

> Heavy cream, sour cream, or yogurt is often added to the filling.

With singular and plural nouns connected by "or," the verb is governed by the noun closest to it.

Rice or potatoes are my recommendation for the neutral-tasting starch this rich sauce calls for.

Potatoes or rice is my recommendation for . . .

Nouns as Verbs

Avoid using nouns as verbs. The following are not all technically incorrect because many of the nouns are also listed as verbs in dictionaries, but the poor examples are nonetheless graceless English.

POOR: Sieve the cottage cheese.
GOOD: Press the cottage cheese through a sieve.

POOR: Juice the lemons.
GOOD: Squeeze the lemons.

POOR: Lid the pot.
GOOD: Cover the pot.

POOR: Portion the soup into four bowls.
GOOD: Ladle the soup into four bowls.

POOR: Plate the food in the kitchen.
GOOD: Arrange the food on plates in the kitchen.

POOR: Julienne the carrots.
GOOD: Cut the carrots into julienne.

POOR: Sauce the pasta.
GOOD: Pour the sauce over the pasta, tossing to combine.

POOR: Butter and sugar a foil collar.
GOOD: Coat a foil collar with butter and lightly sprinkle with sugar.

POOR: Pool (or puddle) the sauce on a serving plate.
GOOD: Spoon a small amount of sauce onto a serving plate.

ADJECTIVES

Adjectives should be in logical sequence. In the following examples, the adjective next to the noun is the key word in identifying the ingredient, and the one or ones preceding it are in descending order of importance.

frozen chopped spinach
grated fresh ginger
fresh ripe tomatoes
canned Italian plum tomatoes
ground roasted cumin seeds
small fresh hot pepper
grated seedless cucumbers
chopped mixed glacé fruit
chilled unsalted butter
unsifted all-purpose flour

Similarly, a logical order of preparation should appear when the adjectives follow the noun.

3 tomatoes, peeled, seeded, and chopped
1 green pepper, cored, seeded, and cut into chunks

PRONOUNS

The question of gender in food writing is a difficult one. The use of *he/she,* although acceptable, tends to be cumbersome and distracting. It is traditional to use *he* and *his* for both sexes, and this practice is followed by many reputable institutions.

The stereotyping of sex roles has been under attack, however, and many publishers have encouraged their writers to avoid the implication that cooking and housework are women's roles. All of this puts the food writer into an interesting quandary. Which is more offensive: to continue to rely on *he* and *him* for both sexes, or to change over to *she* and *her* and thus imply that a woman's place is in the kitchen?

With a little ingenuity, most *he/she* constructions can be avoided:

POOR: While working with spun sugar, the cook would do well to wear her largest apron and tie her hair up in a net.

GOOD: While working with spun sugar, wear your largest apron and cover your hair with a chef's hat.

Pronouns are used to avoid repeating a noun, but this can lead to confusion if the antecedent is in question. When there is any doubt as to which noun a pronoun refers to, repeat the noun. Clarity is more important than elegant construction.

POOR: Cut off the ends of the zucchini and slice them . . .

GOOD: Cut off the ends of the zucchini and slice the zucchini . . .

GOOD: Trim the ends and slice the zucchini . . .

POOR: Its skin needs to be peeled before it can be . . .

GOOD: Its skin needs to be peeled before the ginger can be . . .

GOOD: The ginger needs to be peeled before it can be . . .

A company is referred to as *it,* not *they.*

Clemente Jacques has had to change *its* label . . .

PREPOSITIONS

Many expressions with prepositions are idiomatic and abide by no rule. "In" usually indicates position; "into" indicates motion from without to within.

Beat the eggs *in* the top of a double boiler.
Pour the hot milk *into* the eggs.

But there are idioms with these and other prepositions.

blend *with*
center *in* or *on*
coat *with*

cut *in* half; but cut *into* slices
divide *into*
dredge *in*
parallel *to* or *with*
place *in*
plunge *into*
put *in* or *into*
similar *to*
surround *by*

In the ingredients list, inexact words such as pinch, dash, bunch, drop should be followed by "of."

Pinch of salt
Dash of Tabasco
Bunch of carrots
Drop of vanilla extract

— *Careful Writing and Editing* —

Although we may not be able to state the rules of grammar that govern our speech and writing, we should be able to follow them from having heard correct English and from having read well-crafted and effective writing. It is often helpful to analyze the work of writers one admires, especially food writers in this instance. It is illuminating to see how they convey ideas gracefully and clearly.

Meanwhile, we offer some grammatical guidelines. Many of the poor examples in this section will seem ludicrous, but they have all appeared in published cookbooks, thus proving that if the author is not alert, the editor and copy editor must be.

MODIFIERS

A dangling modifier, usually at the beginning of a sentence, is so-called because it does not modify the word that it seems to.

POOR: Although eaten with rice in Goa, I love to serve these mussels all by themselves as a first course.

GOOD: Although eaten with rice in Goa, these mussels can be served by themselves as a first course.

POOR: When dipped in melted butter or hollandaise, one truly discovers the food of the gods.

GOOD: When dipped in melted butter or hollandaise, these are truly the food of the gods.

POOR: Like other cabbages, do not wash cauliflower before storing.

GOOD: Like other cabbages, cauliflower should not be washed before storing.

POOR: Yet for all their popularity, most people never have cranberries in any other form except cranberry sauce (usually canned).

GOOD: Yet for all their popularity, cranberries are almost never served in any form except cranberry sauce (usually canned).

POOR: Fragrant with spice and gilded with saffron, I like to serve this pretty dish with curries.

GOOD: Fragrant with spice and gilded with saffron, this pretty dish is especially good with curries.

Such words as "only" and "just" should be placed next to the words they modify.

POOR: This just takes a few seconds.

GOOD: This takes just a few seconds.

POOR: If you can only buy ground spices, . . .

GOOD: If you can buy only ground spices, . . .

RESTRICTIVE AND NONRESTRICTIVE CLAUSES

Many good writers choose to ignore the proper use of *which* and *that,* but the rule is so simple that it seems foolish to defy it.

That is used in restrictive clauses—those that are essential to the sense of the sentence. *Which* is used in nonrestrictive clauses—those that are parenthetical to the sense of the sentence and can be dropped without changing the meaning. Nonrestrictive clauses are always preceded by a comma.

RESTRICTIVE: This aromatic mixture incorporates spices that are supposed to heat the body.

This means that the mixture includes only the particular spices that are believed to heat the body. If *that* is changed to *which,* preceded by a comma, the sense would be changed to mean that all spices heat the body.

NONRESTRICTIVE: The cooking liquor is then used to simmer pea beans and corn, which are served alongside.

The *which* clause here simply gives additional information; its inclusion has no effect on the central meaning of the sentence.

COMBINATION: Ricotta is made from whey, which is the watery part of the milk that separates from the curd.

The *which* clause here is descriptive, explaining what whey is. It could be eliminated without changing the meaning of the sentence (Ricotta is made from whey), but the *that* clause is essential.

If in doubt as to which to use, if the clause can be separated from the main part of the sentence by a comma, use *which.*

UNNECESSARY WORDS

Some words in recipes should be dropped because they are redundant and often foolish. Others can be dropped because they are implied and understood in the context.

Redundancy is repetition, producing superfluous words. The words in parentheses in the following examples are redundant and should be eliminated.

Tabasco (sauce)
port (wine)
sherry (wine)
prosciutto (ham)
pizza (pie)
(shrimp) scampi
chorizo (sausage)
cayenne (pepper)

A preposition is often superfluous:

When all (of) the milk has been used . . .
Place half (of) the olives in a bowl with the vinegar . . .

The following words in parentheses are not wrong, but can be dropped because they are implied and understood in the context:

In the Ingredients List

1 pint (fresh) brussels sprouts, or one 10-ounce package frozen (brussels sprouts)
1 tablespoon chopped fresh basil, or 1 teaspoon dried (basil)
1 cup (raw) rice
3 ripe (fresh) tomatoes
2 garlic cloves, (peeled and) minced
6 scallions, (trimmed and) thinly sliced crosswise
1 chili pepper, (halved), seeded, and diced
3 peaches, peeled, (pitted), and chopped

In Instructions and Text

Heat the oil and sauté the onions (in it) until . . .

Cook, (while) stirring with a wooden spatula.

Taste for seasoning and adjust balance of salt and lemon juice (if you need to).

(Now) put in the cauliflower and cook . . .

This dish may be prepared ahead (of time) and re-heated.

Use the beans to weight (down) the pastry shell.

With a little (advance) planning, you can . . .

It is (absolutely) essential that . . .

Reduce the sauce (down) to ½ cup.

If the mushrooms are small (in size), do not quarter them.

Combine (together) the oil, vinegar, garlic, and scal-lions.

You may use (anywhere) from 6 to 8 eggs . . .

Bring to a boil, cover, (reduce heat), and simmer for 10 minutes.

Words used as bridges or transitions—"set aside," "reserve," "meanwhile," "then"—are useful to the food writer in making complicated instructions seem more comprehensible, and in easing the effect of what can seem a series of abrupt commands. They should not be overused, however.

"Set aside" and "reserve" are unnecessary instructions if the ingredient will be used in the next two or three steps. They can be helpful, however, in cases where considerable advance preparation is required, particularly in Asian recipes when the cook should have everything at hand for the final assembly.

HELPFUL: Pick out 6 of the best-looking shrimps and reserve. Chop the rest.

Put the turnips in a bowl and rub them with salt. Set aside for about 2 hours.

Pour boiling water over the mushrooms and soak them for about 15 minutes. Drain, reserving the mushrooms and the liquid. Combine the cornstarch and water and set aside.

Remove the almonds and drain on paper towels. Set them aside until needed for garnish.

UNNECESSARY: Slice the potatoes ½ inch thick, place in a bowl of water (and set aside). Slice the zucchini into ½-inch rounds (and set aside). Slice the onions ½ inch thick (and set aside). When all the vegetables are prepared . . .

Grate 1 pound of carrots, which will yield about 3 cups packed. (Set aside.) Sift the flour . . . Gently stir in the grated carrots.

"Meanwhile" is also an overused word, but there are times when it is helpful in signaling the cook to go on with the preparation while something else is cooking or marinating. Do not use it when what is meant is "next."

HELPFUL: Cook about 20 minutes, or until the potatoes are very tender. Meanwhile, sauté the onion, garlic, and parsley . . .

Cover the beans and cook about 15 minutes, or until tender. Meanwhile, brown the pecans lightly in the butter over low heat.

UNNECESSARY: Roll out the piecrust and place it in the prepared pan. (Meanwhile) assemble the apples, cinnamon, sugar, and lemon juice.

Chop the onions, peppers, parsley, and tomato. (Meanwhile) prepare the beef . . .

The words "then" and "next" are almost always unnecessary.

(Then) carefully fold 7 tablespoons of the sugar into the meringue.

Pour oil into a skillet and sauté the vegetables until tender. (Next) add the beef and . . .

Other Unnecessary Words

About: Do not use when a time range is given because the range itself means that the timing is not exact.

POOR: Cook for about 30 to 40 minutes.
GOOD: Cook for about 35 minutes.
GOOD: Cook for 30 to 40 minutes.

Around

The pan is then shaken (around) until the spices turn a shade or two darker.

Away

The skin needs to be peeled (away) before the ginger can be chopped.

Else

You can take the seeds out of the pods, or (else) you can buy the seeds.

Off

Wash (off) the coconut pieces.
It is best to start (off) with a fresh batch.

Out

Delicious pancakes made (out) of vegetables
This will thin (out) the sauce a little
Measure (out) the dry ingredients
Roll (out) the dough

Together

Mix (together) the molasses, eggs, and vanilla

Up

Add the chopped (up) garlic
Cut them each (up) into 3 or 4 pieces
. . . all ready to heat (up) at a moment's notice
If you have not used it (up) after 4 days . . .
The blades of the beater should be warmed (up) by . . .
Roll (up) into a salami shape
Cook until the mussels open (up)
Heat (up) a heavy iron skillet.
Place the sherbet in the refrigerator to soften (up)
If left in, this will shrink (up) and twist the meat . . .

Exceptions: Some food expressions with "up" are idiomatic and without it mean something slightly different.

1 roasting chicken, cut up
Cook until they puff up
You should end up with a thick red sauce
Break up the lumps . . .

Whether (or not)

When it comes to making apple pie, the most hotly debated controversy is whether (or not) the apples should be cooked before they're put into the crust.

FOREIGN WORDS

The language of recipes is especially rich because it has long embraced foreign words and terms. In America we have tasted the dishes of many immigrants and made them our own. And, of course, culinary terms have come to us from Auguste Escoffier, who codified the rules of haute cuisine.

In the years since Escoffier's death in 1935, chefs and cooks and food writers have added to the language (and broken his rules) through travel and curiosity about many foreign cuisines.

The food writer must, as always, consider his readership when it comes to using foreign words. A recipe for people with more than basic skills can safely use the term "Mornay," whereas one for beginners is better off with "cheese sauce."

Certain verbs from the French, such as deglaze, sauté, and purée, have become accepted and understood in recipe writing. But the writer should avoid translations of French terms that are awkward or unfamiliar in English.

POOR: Sweat the onions (from the French *suer*)
GOOD: Cover the pan and cook the onions over low heat without letting them brown.

POOR: Mount the butter (from *monter le beurre*)
GOOD: Add the butter, a little at a time, swirling the pan . . .

POOR: Nap the veal with the sauce (from *napper*)
GOOD: Spoon the sauce over the veal.

Words that originate in languages with non-Roman alphabets can be transliterated in many ways. Thus we have yogurt, yoghurt, yogourt. If the word is in the dictionary as a standard English word, the author should use that spelling.

yogurt, bulgur, pilaf

If the words are unfamiliar, the author is responsible for submitting an authoritative list of spellings that will then be followed by the copy editor.

When to Italicize

Culinary words enter and are absorbed into the language much faster than dictionaries can be revised. And dictionaries often do not include popular culinary terms. Therefore, we favor roman type for foreign words rather than italic in most cases, and always in the ingredients list, unless, of course, the ingredients list is set in italic.

Stir-fry, al dente, sushi, moussaka, guacamole, feta have been added in recent years to the already fully naturalized American words like sauté, julienne, béarnaise, and bouquet garni. Ratatouille is now such a cliché it comes in a boil-a-bag. Land O Lakes offers Pour-a-Quiche. And the advertisement proclaims "Goya Introduces Tapas," so these Spanish appetizers are right there on supermarket shelves.

There are, of course, exceptions, and these are usually terms that still need to be defined. Minestrone, for example, is a thoroughly Americanized word, but the plural, *minestre,* is not.

> The *minestre* of Italy, the thick vegetable soups that often constitute the evening meal . . .

To sum up, italicize only those words that are not in the dictionary or would be totally foreign to the average cook.

Accents

Proper spelling of foreign words includes the accents, particularly those that govern pronunciation. Some words have lost their accents through frequent use in English (for example, crepe), and dictionaries are omitting many more or listing accented words as a second preference. But we urge both writers and editors to make an exception to dictionary style, especially Webster's Third.

We don't want a generation of young people pronouncing purée "purEE," and in some cases the accents can change the meaning of a word. Pâte, without the accent over the final "e," is the French term for pastry or batter (pâte à choux, pâte brisée). Pâté, with the final accent, is the ground meat or vegetable terrine. Similarly, glace, without an accent, means ice cream; glacé, with the final accent, means frozen or glazed, as a cake.

French, the foreign language most commonly used in cooking, is profusely accented. French words carry five kinds of accent, all governing pronunciation: the acute (sauté), the grave (crème), the circumflex (entrecôte), the cedilla (niçoise), and the diaeresis (Noël, poële).

Italian has two accents that affect pronunciation: the grave (caffè) and the circumflex (caôda).

Spanish also has two: the acute, which governs emphasis (plátanos), and the tilde, which governs pronunciation (jalapeño).

German has only the umlaut, which governs pronunciation (spätzle). Some publications add an "e" to the vowel when the umlaut is omitted (spaetzle), but since almost every printing facility has the umlaut, this is unnecessary.

For accent marks in other languages whose accenting systems are unfamiliar, the writer must be careful to submit a carefully accented manuscript that the editors will follow.

Publishing houses and publications vary as to whether recipe titles printed in capital letters are accented, but since neither the writer nor the copy editor knows in advance how the book will be designed and whether the title will be all caps or upper and lower case, the accents should be clearly indicated.

CHOICE OF WORDS

Confusing Terms

The writer should say what he means and not fall back on meaningless culinary terms that either no longer apply or never did.

DAY-OLD BREAD

Unless the author specifies freshly made French or Italian bread, which dries out after a day, this is a meaningless term today. Commercially made bread is often more than a day old when it is bought, and it retains its freshness for several days. Stale bread, which is another term frequently used, sounds as if the bread is moldy. It is best to specify dried bread, telling the cook to dry it in the oven if necessary.

MARINATE OVERNIGHT

This makes it sound as if the lamb that has been marinating must be cooked first thing in the morning, which is seldom the case. It is clearer to specify a time: Marinate 8 to 12 hours, or whatever.

DIJON-STYLE MUSTARD

Dijon is a style of mustard, based on a French formula using mustard seed, vinegar, white wine, and spices. It is a mild mustard and should be called Dijon mustard whether it is made in Connecticut or France.

BEAT THE EGG YOLKS UNTIL THICK AND LEMON-COLORED

This is an instruction that is used in hundreds of recipes and is misleading. What is called for is to beat the egg yolks until slightly thickened and paler yellow.

BEAT THE EGG WHITES UNTIL STIFF

If they are stiff, according to Marion Cunningham, they're overbeaten. She prefers "until they stand in soft peaks."

Similarly, avoid old-fashioned terms.

POOR: If it starts to catch, turn the heat down.
GOOD: If it starts to stick, turn the heat down.

POOR: Plump the raisins.
GOOD: Soak the raisins in the cider for about 10 minutes, until they are plump.

POOR: Purge the eggplant.
GOOD: Sprinkle salt over the eggplant slices and let drain for about an hour to remove excess water.

New Terms

New terms are constantly coming into the language of recipes because of new equipment. Most of them will probably be with us for many years.

FOOD PROCESSOR

Process

Drop in eggs and egg yolks and process with one or two bursts until blended.

Pulse

Put the grapes in a food processor in three batches and pulse just until coarsely chopped.

Mince the onion and parsley together by pulsing the motor on and off about five times.

Feed Tube

With the processor running, pour liquid through the feed tube in a steady stream.

Slice the potatoes by pushing them lightly down the feed tube of a food processor fitted with the slicing disk.

MICROWAVE OVEN

We now have a new verb and adjective in the language of recipes, but don't overdo them.

Microwave as a verb

Eggplant retains a beautiful green color when it is microwaved.

Microwaving vegetables retains their color, texture, and vitamins.

Microwave as an adjective

Cover tightly with microwave-safe plastic wrap.

Use any microwavable dish as long as the sides are at least 2 inches high.

Miscellaneous

Cook at High for 5 minutes.
Cook at 100% for 15 minutes.

PRESSURE COOKER

Seal the cooker, bring to 10 pounds pressure, and cook 15 minutes per pound.

Maintain the pressure throughout processing at 10 pounds, raising or lowering the heat as needed.

Only tough old birds should be pressure cooked; young tender ones will fall to pieces.

POTS AND PANS

Nonstick surface

Noncorrosive, nonaluminum, nonreactive

INSTANT-READING THERMOMETER

After 25 minutes, test the internal temperature of the beef by inserting an instant-reading thermometer in the thickest portion.

Interchangeable Words and Terms

When more than one word or term describes the same thing, a cook can be confused if both terms appear in the same recipe or book.

INGREDIENTS:

Broth/Stock. Interchangeable. Stock usually refers to the home-made product and broth to the canned (it is called chicken or beef broth on all cans). In Italian and Spanish, the word is always "broth."

Unsalted Butter/Sweet Butter. Interchangeable. Unsalted is preferred because it is unmistakable, and that is how it is generally labeled.

Hot Red Pepper Flakes/Crushed Red Pepper. Interchangeable. Asian markets usually sell the former, supermarkets the latter.

Scallion/Green Onion. Technically these are two different stages of the common onion. A scallion is a shoot that is pulled before the bulb is formed. A green onion is a shoot with a definite bulb formation. Scallion has become the general term for both in most areas of the country, but not all.

Jerusalem Artichoke/Sunchoke. Interchangeable. The latter is a new marketing term for the former.

Light or Thin Soy Sauce/Dark or Black Soy Sauce. Most authentic Chinese cookbooks use "thin" and "black." But many commercial brands of soy sauce available in supermarkets are labeled "light" and "dark."

Coarse Salt/Kosher Salt. Interchangeable.

Dry Mustard/Powdered Mustard. Interchangeable.

Artichoke Heart/Artichoke Bottom. Used interchangeably, but a heart consists of a portion of the bottom with a few small tender leaves. (Commercially packaged artichoke hearts usually come from tiny California artichokes that have almost no choke.) An artichoke bottom refers to the meaty round base of the vegetable without the leaves and choke.

Hazelnut/Filbert. Interchangeable. Hazelnut is preferred (it grows on the hazel tree). Filbert is technically the European variety.

Lemon Zest/Lemon Rind. Zest is the thin, colored, outside part of the rind. The rind includes the zest and the white pithy layer next to the fruit.

Hard-Boiled Egg/Hard-Cooked Egg. Interchangeable.

Green Beans/String Beans/Snap Beans. Interchangeable. Green beans is preferred by growers and plant breeders, who long ago produced virtually stringless beans.

Pine Nuts/Pignoli. Interchangeable.

Heavy Cream/Whipping Cream. There apparently is a hairline difference between these two kinds of cream, but they are used interchangeably. The labeling is regional.

Cayenne/Ground Red Pepper. Years ago, the spice industry started to phase out the term "cayenne" in favor of "red pepper," but that doesn't seem to have happened. Cayenne is still available and labeled as such on supermarket shelves. It is properly called "cayenne," not "cayenne pepper," which is redundant.

Candied Ginger/Crystallized Ginger. Interchangeable.

Confectioners' Sugar/Powdered Sugar. Interchangeable, but boxes are labeled "confectioners' sugar."

UTENSILS AND EQUIPMENT:

Baking Dish/Baking Pan. Used interchangeably. The word "dish" implies glass, porcelain, or enamel-coated cast iron. "Pan" implies metal, such as stainless steel or aluminum.

Baking Sheet/Cookie Sheet/Jelly Roll Pan. Baking sheet and cookie sheet are used interchangeably to describe a flat pan (traditionally of carbon steel, but more recently with a nonstick surface) either with no sides or with sides no higher than ½ inch so heat circulates freely. A jelly roll pan has sides about 1 inch high to prevent batter from spilling over.

Casserole/Dutch Oven. Casseroles are enamel-coated cast iron, treated glass, or porcelain pans with tight-fitting covers. A Dutch oven is usually black cast iron.

Frying Pan/Skillet/Sauté Pan. Used interchangeably. Frying pan and skillet often refer to cast-iron pans, but they can also be nonstick. Frying pans made of black steel are also used for sautéing. Frying pans and skillets have sloping sides about 2 inches high. A sauté pan technically has straight sides about 3 inches high to keep food from jumping out as it slides back and forth across the burner. Many chefs and food writers refer to sauté pans as skillets (but not as frying pans).

TROUBLESOME WORDS

The following are general (not just cooking) terms that writers and editors often find troublesome.

About/Approximately: Interchangeable, but why use a thirteen-letter word when a five-letter word says the same thing?

Alternately: First one then the other.
Alternatively: One instead of the other.

Add the melted chocolate alternately with the butter.

Alternatively, you can use powdered cocoa.

Affect: To influence, change, or pretend.
Effect: To accomplish, complete (noun is almost always effect).

> This will affect the texture of the ice cream.
>
> Any chilies that go bad should be thrown away, as they will affect the whole batch.
>
> Pyrex and stainless steel baking pans are best because they do not affect the taste of the sauce.
>
> The whole effect is very colorful and dramatic.

Complement: Complete, serve to make whole.
Compliment: Express admiration, flatter.

> Fried eggplant and a yogurt dish would complement the meat well.
>
> You will be complimented on your inventiveness when you serve this dish.

Continually: Over and over again; lasts with pauses or breaks.
Continuously: Unbroken; without pauses or breaks.

> Process continuously if you want a smooth butter.
>
> The stock should be boiling continuously as the corn meal is stirred in.
>
> Stir continually to prevent the sauce from sticking.

Farther: Physical distance.
Further: Extent or degree; additional or continued.

> The farther you have to walk, the less efficient the kitchen.
>
> The further you explore the cuisines of Asia, the greater your rewards.

Fewer: Used of numbers.
Less: Used of quantity.

If you prefer fewer calories, substitute yogurt for the mayonnaise.

Shape the mixture into little hamburgers; you should have no fewer than 20.

Use less salt if canned chicken broth is substituted for homemade.

Healthful: Promoting health.
Healthy: Having health.

A healthful diet makes healthy people.

Place: Denotes greater care or exactness
Put: More general term

Place the berries on a baking sheet in a single layer and put them in the freezer.

Put the plums in a heavy saucepan with the sugar, currant jelly, and cinnamon stick.

Place the apple slices around the tart shell in a neat pattern.

Preceding: Immediately before, without interval.
Previous: Going before at any time or in any order.

Trim the artichokes according to the preceding recipe.

Clean the squid according to instructions in the previous chapter.

Sit/Stand: These seem to be interchangeable.

Turn off the heat and let the pan sit for a while.

Allow the clams to stand in cold water until they disgorge their sand.

Add yeast to warm water and let sit 5 minutes.

Unique: The only one of its kind.

There are no degrees of uniqueness—no "very unique," no "most unique." Just "unique." And there are few things in the world that fit the definition of unique, so the writer should save this word until it is appropriate.

—3—

Punctuation

PROPER PUNCTUATION IS VITAL for clarity and the smooth flow of sentences. Too much punctuation creates choppy sentences that are annoying to read and difficult to follow; too little punctuation can lead to ambiguity and sometimes to misinterpretation. The writer and the editor must know a few rules of punctuation, and otherwise use common sense to avoid confusion of meaning.

—*Period*—

Periods are used in recipes for the normal functions of ending declarative sentences and with dollars and cents, titles, ellipsis, and some abbreviations. There are also times when a period is or is not used that apply especially to recipe writing.

WITH RUN-IN HEADINGS

A period can be used in place of a colon after a side heading, one that is printed on the same line as the text.

> *Skinning filberts.* Spread the shelled nuts on a baking sheet . . .

WITH NUMERALS

Numerals are followed by periods when the number opens a paragraph in the instructions.

1. Line the pan with the prepared pastry.

WITH ABBREVIATIONS

Use periods for the following:

Weights and measures—1 doz., 3 lbs., 6-in. strip, 2 Tbsp.
Sizes—No. 2 can, No. 7 pastry tube

Omit periods for the following:

Common food or dietary abbreviations—MSG (monosodium glutamate, RDA (recommended dietary allowance), USDA (United States Department of Agriculture), CIA (Culinary Institute of America)
Metric weights and measures—3 g, 1 dl, 2 kg
Temperatures—Heat the oil until it reaches 450°F (232°C) on a deep-fat thermometer

WITH RECIPE COMPONENTS

Omit periods for the following:

At the end of a recipe title
At the end of a line in the ingredients list and at the end of the last line in the list
At the end of a parenthetical statement in the ingredients list, even if it is a complete sentence

1 cup mashed potatoes (instant mashed potatoes can be used)

After the yield line
Serves 4
Yield: 4 servings
Makes 1½ cups

— Comma —

A comma is used to indicate a slight pause, to separate things in a series, to place things in apposition, to set off a subordinate clause when it opens the sentence, and to set off parenthetical information.

In general, the fewer commas the better, because they tend to clutter the page and to slow down the reader. Some commas, however, are critical.

IN INGREDIENTS LIST

With Preparation Information

Use a comma to separate the ingredient and the preparation.

½ cup pine nuts, toasted in the oven
2 tomatoes, peeled, seeded, and chopped
6 red new potatoes, scrubbed
5 ounces goat cheese, chilled and cut into ¼-inch slices
1 striped bass, cleaned but with head left on

With Descriptive Material

Use a comma to separate descriptive material from the ingredient.

4 slices of ginger, about the size of a quarter
1 large roasting chicken, about 4 pounds
4 soft ripe pears, preferably Anjou
1 tablespoon butter, softened
1½ cups chopped leeks, both white and green part
6 black olives, preferably Italian
1 tablespoon mild-flavored honey, such as acacia or clover

A comma may be used to separate such asides as "optional" and "see page 333" in the ingredients list, although parentheses are preferable.

With Multiple Adjectives

Separate two or more adjectives by commas if each modifies the noun alone.

3 quarts cleaned, well-scrubbed mussels
1½ pounds skinless, boneless flounder
2 cups cored, skinned, cubed tomatoes

If there is a long string of adjectives and too many commas seem to be required, perhaps the solution is to eliminate some of the adjectives or to reword the ingredient.

POOR: 36 pitted, whole, soft, black olives, preferably French
GOOD: 36 pitted black olives, preferably French

POOR: 1 small, ripe, unblemished avocado
GOOD: 1 small ripe avocado

POOR: 1 pound red, new, waxy potatoes
GOOD: 1 pound red new potatoes

POOR: ¾ cup finely chopped, cored, seeded, sweet green pepper
GOOD: ¾ cup finely chopped green pepper
GOOD: 1 large green pepper, cored, seeded, and finely chopped

If the first adjective modifies the idea expressed by the succeeding adjectives and the noun, no comma should be used. The underlined portion is one thought, modified by the adjective that precedes it.

4 large stuffed green olives
1 pint ripe but firm cherry tomatoes
2 pints shucked raw oysters
6 large ripe tomatoes
½ cup fine fresh bread crumbs
12 firm white mushrooms
1 cup diced cooked ham

½ cup small black olives
1 large red Italian onion
2 cups canned Italian plum tomatoes
3 tablespoons freshly grated imported Parmesan cheese
2 cups chopped green or red bell peppers
1 dried hot red pepper
1 cup unsweetened frozen orange juice concentrate

With Alternative Ingredients

If alternative ingredients have different measurements, separate them by a comma. There is no need to emphasize the word "or" by italicizing or capitalizing it.

1 tablespoon chopped fresh basil, or 1 teaspoon dried
3 heads Bibb lettuce, or 1 head Boston
3 shallots, or 1 small onion
¼ teaspoon cayenne, or ½ teaspoon hot pepper flakes
5 artichokes, or 1 (9-ounce) package frozen artichoke hearts
1 tablespoon safflower oil, or 2 tablespoons vegetable oil
½ cup coarsely grated fresh horseradish, or ⅓ cup drained bottled horseradish
20 biscotti, or enough crumbled melba toast to make 2 cups

If the amount of the alternative ingredient is the same, do not use a comma.

1 tablespoon chopped parsley or chervil
4 tablespoons butter or margarine
½ teaspoon crushed saffron threads or ground turmeric
½ cup Calvados or applejack

IN A SERIES

Many publishing houses insist on what is called the serial comma—a comma used to separate each element in a series of three or more elements, including the one immediately preceding the conjunction: butter, sugar, and salt. Many newspapers and periodicals do not follow this style and it is frequently a matter of personal habit and preference.

Nevertheless, the serial comma can be useful in recipe writing—often a needed aid to clarity—in a series of phrases, clauses, or instructional stages.

Serial commas optional:

Mix the peppers with the chicken, potatoes, and peas.

Trim, peel, and wash the fennel.

Combine the cornstarch, soy sauce, and mustard.

Serial commas helpful:

When all the lamb is brown, return earlier batches to the pan, raise the heat, add the wine, and cook for 3 minutes.

Put the crisped pancetta in a large salad bowl, add the salad greens and the scallion, and sprinkle lightly with salt and pepper.

Remove the pans from the oven, put them on a rack to cool, and loosen the layers by running a knife around the insides of the pans.

WITH PARENTHETICAL PHRASES AND ADVERBIAL CLAUSES

Set off parenthetical phrases and adverbial clauses with commas.

With the motor running, add the oil in a steady stream.

Add the chilled butter, 1 tablespoon at a time, and whisk . . .

Cook the sauce, stirring frequently, until it is thick.

Place the chicken, skin side down, in the skillet.

If there is too much liquid, remove it with a bulb baster.

When the flames die down, add the tomatoes and fish stock.

As with all seafood stews, the fish goes into the pot at the very end so it does not overcook.

If the writer prefers to start a sentence with the pan or utensil information, the phrase should be set off by a comma. If, as is preferable, it follows the verb and noun, no comma is needed.

In a small bowl, combine the miso, honey, and spices.
Combine the miso, honey, and spices in a small bowl.

In a large saucepan, bring the stock to a boil.
Bring the stock to a boil in a large saucepan.

If there are too many short phrases or clauses in one sentence, and therefore too many commas, it's time to rewrite.

POOR: Cook, covered, over medium heat, until leeks are slightly limp, about 10 minutes.
GOOD: Cover and cook over medium heat until leeks are slightly limp, about 10 minutes.

POOR: In a heavy deep saucepan, heat enough oil to measure 1½ inches to 375°F and in it fry rounded teaspoons of the dough in batches for 3 to 4 minutes, or until they are puffed and golden, transferring them with a slotted spoon as they are fried to paper towels.
GOOD: Pour 1½ inches of oil into a deep heavy saucepan and heat to 375°F. Fry rounded teaspoons of the dough in batches for 3 to 4 minutes, or until they are puffed and golden. Transfer them with a slotted spoon to paper towels to drain.

POOR: In a large heatproof bowl, using a wire whisk, beat together all the filling ingredients except the butter.

GOOD: In a large heatproof bowl, whisk together all the filling ingredients except the butter.

WITH TESTS FOR DONENESS

Use a comma to separate the suggested cooking time from a description of how the dish should look or feel.

> Bake for 30 minutes, or until a knife inserted midway between the rim and center comes out clean.
>
> Cook the lamb at a very gentle simmer until it is fork-tender, about 1 hour.
>
> Boil gently, without stirring, until it is thickened and smooth, 8 or 9 minutes.
>
> Broil about 5 minutes, until quail are golden brown.

WITH APPOSITIVES

Commas are generally used to place things in apposition, or to define or further explain them. Dashes or parentheses may also be used, depending on the sentence and the emphasis desired.

> One that was unforgettable consisted of borschok, a ruby-red, beet-flavored clear consommé, and seven kinds of piroshki, those delicious Russian pastries.
>
> Pass the soup through a chinois, the French cone-shaped strainer.
>
> Couscous, a kind of semolina, is daily fare in North Africa.
>
> Mention veal shanks and thoughts inevitably turn to osso buco, braised veal shanks with vegetables.

The conjunction "or" is sometimes used with the appositive. In this case the comma is essential to make it clear that the two things are the same, not a choice. Parentheses may also be used, omitting "or."

2 pounds monkfish, or bellyfish
4 small mirlitons, or chayote squash

WITH NUMBERS

No comma is used with weights and measures.

A fish weighing 1 pound 3 ounces
Contents of a 1-pound-4-ounce can of stewed tomatoes

Use a comma to separate two unrelated numbers coming together, or better yet, rewrite.

To serve 8, 3 dozen will be necessary.
You will need 3 dozen to serve 8.

WITH OMISSIONS

A comma can be used to indicate the omission of a word or words.

The French call it *fenouil,* the Germans, *Fenchel,* the Italians, *finocchio,* the Spanish, *hinojo.*

— Semicolon —

IN COMPOUND SENTENCES

A semicolon indicates a lesser break than a period. Use it in compound sentences where the main clauses are closely connected in sense.

> The canned clams are sufficiently salty; do not add more salt before you've tasted the completed dish.
>
> Place the tomato slices on the fish; sprinkle the fillets with green pepper and onion.
>
> The pasta and vegetables can be prepared ahead, as can the sauce; combine shortly before serving.
>
> Bake in the center of the preheated oven for 10 minutes; the bagels should be set but not browned.

WITH CONJUNCTIVE ADVERBS

Use a semicolon before such conjunctive adverbs as thus, otherwise, however—that is, to introduce a related sentence that offers additional or correlated information.

> The chef suggests using a Jaffa orange for the garnish; however, any other type of orange will do.
>
> Remove from the heat promptly; otherwise the meat will toughen.

IN A SERIES

A semicolon is useful in dividing a complicated series, particularly after a colon.

> The technique is simple: Sauté onion in oil until it is very tender; add rice and sauté until the edges of the grains turn transparent; add hot liquid gradually, allowing it to be absorbed before adding the next measure.

— Colon —

WITH LISTS

A colon is used to introduce a list or series.

> It is then poached with an assortment of winter vegetables: leeks, carrots, celery, and brussels sprouts.

> You can significantly reduce the salt content of the following foods by soaking them for 15 minutes in cold water: anchovies, capers, feta cheese, and sauerkraut or other pickled vegetables.

> Anything goes as an underlayer for the mashed potatoes: green peas or beans, lima beans, diced turnips, sliced celery.

WITH INTRODUCTORY COPY

A colon is used to emphasize a sequence of thought between two clauses or to introduce an illustration or amplification of the first. Note that the second element begins with a capital letter if it consists of a complete sentence. Otherwise it is lowercased.

> These dishes illustrate a key point in cooking: A little imagination in ingredient combinations can dress up everyday dishes so they become memorable.

> The sauce will enliven a wide range of desserts: Spoon it over ice cream, pudding, or cream puffs, or dress up sliced plain cake with a dollop of it.

WITH RUN-IN HEADINGS

Use a colon (or a period) following an instructional or side heading.

> *Make the sauce:* Melt the butter . . .

> *To serve:* Place one tortilla on each plate . . .

Kasha Varnitchkes: Follow the recipe for kasha, stirring in 1 cup cooked bowtie noodles just before serving.

Note: It's fine to use commercial mayonnaise for this, but try to find one that's not sweetened.

— *Hyphen* —

IN COMPOUND WORDS

A hyphen is used to link many compound words, although once a word comes into common usage it frequently becomes a solid compound. Check the Word List (Chapter 10), or follow the style of Webster's Third Unabridged or Ninth New Collegiate Dictionary.

Some compounds that are still generally hyphenated:

chick-pea	chock-full
crisp-tender	deep-fry
fork-tender	freeze-dried
stir-fry	half-moons

Many French words are hyphenated:

bain-marie	pot-au-feu
chou-fleur	vol-au-vent

WITH COMPOUND ADJECTIVES

Compound adjectives are usually hyphenated when they precede the noun, particularly when the adjective is a phrase.

deep-dish potpie	double-acting baking powder
ready-to-cook squab	all-purpose flour
black-eyed peas	bite-size pieces
after-dinner coffee	medium-size bowl
fine-mesh sieve	hard-shell clams
Persian-style rice	well-scrubbed mussels
sweet-smelling cantaloupe	hot-and-sour soup

The hyphen is unnecessary in the following compounds because they are two words so closely associated that they form a single concept, and it is this single concept that modifies the noun.

red wine vinegar	whole wheat flour
sour cream cake	lemon meringue pie
chocolate chip cookies	orange juice concentrate
maple syrup frosting	graham cracker crust
devil's food cake	poppy seed straws
health food store	celery root salad

Do not hyphenate compound adjectives that include adverbs ending in *ly*.

finely chopped onions	freshly ground pepper
lightly floured surface	frequently used ingredients

Do not hyphenate proper adjectives unless the hyphen is integral to the term.

Near Eastern	Tex-Mex
southern Italian	Parmigiano-Reggiano

WITH COMPOUND NOUNS

Use a hyphen to connect a compound consisting of two nouns of equal value.

cook-host   restaurant-bar

TO REPLACE "AND"

In recipe titles, a hyphen is often used to replace the word *and.*

Strawberry-Rhubarb Pie	Fudge-Nut Brownies
Coffee-Orange Granité	Cornmeal-Pumpkin Muffins
Broccoli-Leek Purée	

When one or both of the two elements are in themselves compounds, use an en dash (slightly longer than a hyphen) to separate them. (See page 98.)

WITH PREFIXES AND SUFFIXES

Most prefixes and suffixes quickly become solid compounds, but there are exceptions and the careful writer and editor should check the dictionary.

Usually no hyphen:

bone:	backbone, breastbone, wishbone
like:	custardlike, rootlike, nutlike (exceptions: words ending in ll, and frequently l—shell-like, caramel-like)
non:	nonoily, nonaluminum, nonstick
over:	overcook, overripe, overbeat
pre:	precook, preheat
re:	reheat, rearrange, redistribute (exceptions: when a solid compound would cause confusion between two different meanings—re-form, re-create)
semi:	semiliquid, semisolid, semisweet

Usually hyphenated before the noun:

old:	old-fashioned, old-time, old-world
self:	self-cleaning, self-service, self-taught
well:	well-made, well-appointed, well-done

The word "type" is not a suffix and is not considered acceptable as such. If you must use the word, it should be followed by "of."

Many pasta makers prefer the long slim European type of rolling pin.

POOR: In a large casserole-type pot . . .
GOOD: In a large casserole . . .

POOR: This is a hearty stew-type dish . . .
GOOD: This is a hearty stew . . .
GOOD: This dish is like a hearty stew . . .

WITH NUMBERS

Hyphenate adjective compounds formed with a number.

Cut the peppers into 1-inch dice
a 2-quart soufflé dish
three-bean salad
½-inch-thick slices
an 8½ by 5 by 3½-inch pan

Fractions used as adjectives are hyphenated when they are spelled out, which is infrequently in recipes.

fill the pan two-thirds full
one-third cup (usually ⅓ cup)

Do not confuse a numerical adjective and a noun with a fraction. No hyphen should be used in the following examples.

add one quarter of the broccoli
layer one third of the rice in the dish

AWKWARD HYPHENATION

Reword titles and phrases that contain awkward hyphenation.

POOR: Fruit- and Cheese-Topped Coffee Cake
GOOD: Fruit-Topped Coffee Cake
GOOD: Coffee Cake with Fruit and Cheese Topping

POOR: paper-towel-lined plate
GOOD: plate lined with paper towels

POOR: 8- or 9-inch pie plate
GOOD: 8-inch or 9-inch pie plate

There are several sizes of dash, ranging from the hyphen (the shortest) to the 3-em dash (the longest). In between is the 1-em dash, so-called after a unit of type measurement, the em. Since this is the dash most commonly used, we will refer to it hereafter as a regular dash. The en dash, half the size of a regular dash, is almost imperceptibly larger than a hyphen and is ignored by most newspapers and many periodicals. It appears most often in book composition.

An en dash is typed as a hyphen and a regular dash is typed with two or three hyphens in a row. They are marked by the copy editor as $\frac{1}{N}$ and $\frac{1}{M}$. (A typed hyphen is not marked for the compositor except when clarity is in doubt. The copy-editing mark for a hyphen is $=$.)

EN DASH

With Numbers

An en dash is sometimes used to replace the word "to" in inclusive numbers, although "to" is easier to read and more attractive on the page.

> 1–1½ teaspoons Dijon mustard
> 4–5 servings
> Simmer for 10–12 minutes
> See the discussion of cake making on pages 333–34.

In indexes, an en dash is always used with inclusive numbers.

> Bread baking, 333–34
> Puff pastry, 33–34

With Compounds

An en dash is sometimes used to replace the word "and" in compound adjectives, one element of which contains two words. Again, the word "and" is usually easier to read and more attractive on the page.

Macadamia Nut–Coconut Tart
Winter Melon–Rice Salad
ground almond–chocolate mixture
Maple Syrup–Sunflower Seed Bread
Apple–Sour Cream Pie

REGULAR DASH

With a Parenthetical Expression

Use regular dashes to set off a defining or parenthetical element of a sentence.

> Dried bean dishes—lamb with lentils, dried cod with chick-peas, navy bean soup—lend themselves perfectly to one-pot cooking.
>
> It should be served at room temperature with a sauce—I particularly like spinach sauce—and a mixed salad.
>
> We tend to equate coconut with sweets—candies, cakes, custards, and pies—and yet it is integral to dozens of savory dishes, too.
>
> Two strong flavors—smoky eggplant and lemon-sharpened tahini—make an exciting marriage of taste in this Middle Eastern favorite.

In Place of a Comma

A regular dash can be used in place of a comma for emphasis, but if it is used too often, the emphasis will be lost.

> This is an excellent sauce—a good example of how a creamy sauce can be made without cream.
>
> It is loaded with nutrients and low in calories—about 100 a serving.

> I make the soup with sea legs—a Japanese imitation of king crab legs made from fish that is reconstituted and rolled.
>
> This is another recipe where the crabs—like the lobster on page 333—give their flavor to the pasta and then can be eaten as a second course.

A dash may be used before "that is" when the explanation needs more highlighting than a comma provides.

> Cut it into ½-inch slices on the bias—that is, against the grain of the meat—and then into ½-inch cubes.
>
> When butter is clarified—that is, when the milk solids in it are separated and discarded—it does not burn as easily as regular melted butter.

A dash (or parentheses) *must* be used instead of commas when the appositive might be misread as part of the comma series.

POOR: The salad is preceded by consommé madrilène, a tomato soup that may be served hot or chilled, and whole wheat muffins with chives.

GOOD: The salad is preceded by consommé madrilène—a tomato soup that may be served hot or chilled—and whole wheat muffins with chives.

In Place of a Colon

A dash can be used in the sentences on page 93 in place of the colon.

— Quotation Marks —

Quotation marks can be an aid to comprehension and clarity in food writing. Their overuse, however, produces self-conscious writing and should be avoided.

WITH UNUSUAL TERMS

When a word is used in some sense other than its normal one, it can be set apart with quotation marks—especially if the sense would be confusing without them.

> If it is refrigerated, chocolate will "sweat" when it warms to room temperature.
>
> The citric acid in lime juice "cooks" the seafood.
>
> Paper produces a "dry" steam, which makes it good for fish.

If a word or phrase has long been familiar in the context, and is in fact covered by a dictionary definition, quotation marks are not necessary.

> Wash and scrub the mussels and pull away the beards.
>
> Peel the pineapple and cut out the eyes.
>
> Bake the pie shell blind.
>
> Italian rice has more tooth than American rice.

WITH TRANSLATIONS

The English translation of a foreign word or phrase is usually quoted.

> Waterzooi, which means "water on the boil," is . . .
>
> They are manufactured in China and sold as "bean threads" or "glass noodles."

> *Les tous nus,* "the naked ones," are sausages without casings, a Provençal specialty.

IN PLACE OF "SO-CALLED"

Quotation marks can be used where the words "so-called" are omitted.

> There are a dozen "authentic" recipes for succotash.
>
> All kinds of raw and leftover cooked vegetable peelings can go into a stock. But if you want a "standard" recipe, here it is.

WITH CHAPTER TITLES

Use quotation marks when referring to chapters or subsections in a book.

> 1 cup dried black olives (see "Essential Ingredients")
> 1 pound squid, cleaned (see instructions in "Cleaning Fish")
> See Chapter 7, "Dishes from the Master Chefs."

— *Parentheses* —

Parentheses are used to set off digressions—explanations, definitions, cross-references—where commas and dashes would not be sufficient. A parenthetical insertion is usually a departure from the main thrust of the sentence.

WITH EDITORIAL INTERPOLATIONS

Use parentheses to enclose editorial interpolations in the ingredients list and in instructions.

In the ingredients list:

> 4 pounds chicken parts (necks, backs, legs, and thighs)
> 1½ cups chopped leeks (white part only)
> 1½ pounds bay scallops (whole) or sea scallops (quartered)
> 2 tablespoons chopped fresh herbs (parsley, chervil, chives)

In the instructions:

> Pull the meat back (it will be inside out now) and chop off the bone.
>
> Reheat gently until light and creamy (it won't thicken).

Occasionally a reassurance or warning to the cook can be enclosed in parentheses in the ingredients list; it can be a brief sentence, but should not begin with a capital letter or end with a period.

> 3 tablespoons baking soda (this is correct)
>
> 4 hot peppers, seeded and sliced (wear rubber gloves)
>
> 2 tablespoons snipped fresh dill (omit if fresh dill is not available; do not use dried dill)

FOR BRIEF DEFINITIONS

Use parentheses to enclose brief definitions.

> ½ cup bharat (a mixture of ground cinnamon and dried rosebuds)
>
> 3 lumps of sour salt (citric acid)
>
> 6 cups Japanese soup stock (dashi)
>
> 3 pounds leaf lard (pork kidney fat)
>
> Remove the fell (the thin, transparent membrane) and as much of the fat as possible

TO EXPRESS MEASUREMENTS

Use parentheses when measurements are expressed in more than one way.

> 2 cups (1 pound) ricotta cheese
> ½ pound (12 sheets) phyllo pastry
> 1 (7½-ounce) can artichoke hearts
>
> Divide into ten equal portions (about ⅓ cup each).
>
> Add a generous splash (2 to 4 tablespoons) of vinegar to each pan.

FOR PRONUNCIATION

Use parentheses to enclose pronunciations.

> Rillettes (pronounced ree-yet) are . . .

FOR CROSS-REFERENCES

Use parentheses to refer the reader to some other part of the book or article, whether in the ingredients list or the instructions.

> Georgian coriander stew (page 333)
> 1 pound squid, cleaned (see instructions, page 333)
> 1 cup béarnaise sauce (see following recipe)
>
> Char the peppers according to the directions for roasted peppers (page 333).

—*Exclamation Point*—

The exclamation point has one use only: after a true exclamation. If the author wants to arouse enthusiasm or excitement, he has to write an enthusiastic or exciting sentence. An ordinary statement is not made exciting by ending it with an exclamation point.

POOR: This dish is terribly easy and delicious enough to serve at a dinner party!

Make plenty of these and you will be loved by all!

Every Italian restaurant has this on the menu, usually served with meatballs. It still is a good idea!

BETTER: Talk about winners! This was the favorite of all my tasters.

That must have been some dish of lentils!

How clever is the Chinese cook!

— Special Symbols —

Special symbols, which are sometimes considered a form of punctuation, are discussed in Chapter 8, "Format and Typography."

—4—

Numbers

IN RECIPE WRITING, as in scientific and technical writing, it is customary to express numbers in figures rather than to write them out. This is for clarity, not to save space. The graphic immediacy of a numeral leaps to the eye far more quickly than does a written-out number.

Food writing is usually informal, however, and recipes are often interrupted by text, so the writer and editor may adopt a modified numbers style for narrative portions of the copy.

IN TITLES

Spell out numbers used in recipe titles.

Three-Bean Salad
Pasta with Three Cheeses
Chicken with Forty Cloves of Garlic
Seven-Minute Frosting

IN THE INGREDIENTS LIST

Use figures throughout.

1 (8-ounce) can tomato sauce
2 cups heavy cream
2 green peppers, cut into ½-inch dice

1½ cups confectioners' sugar
3 tablespoons cold milk
2 tomatoes, chopped (about 1 cup)
1 cup basil leaves plus 36 perfect leaves, all washed
4 cups thinly sliced cabbage (1½ pounds)
6 baking potatoes, sliced ⅛ inch thick
1 (3½-pound) chicken

IN INSTRUCTIONS

Use figures in recipe instructions for ingredient quantities, times, dimensions, and degrees.

> Add 2 cups of the cabbage and cook slowly until transparent, about 5 minutes.
>
> Pour and scrape the batter into a buttered 9-inch square baking pan and sprinkle the remaining ¾ cup of chopped nuts on top.
>
> Bake at 375 degrees for 20 minutes, or until light brown.
>
> Place 1 basil leaf and 5 or 6 quenelles in each of 12 bouillon cups.

Spell out isolated numbers used in a general sense. This rule holds for recipe instructions as well as text.

> Cut in the butter with two knives
>
> Tie together with two lengths of string
>
> Use the large holes of a four-sided grater
>
> Shake the casserole two or three times
>
> Fold with a figure-eight action
>
> Holding the cake in one hand

Some numbers can be spelled out or used as figures; just be consistent. The parenthetical forms represent alternatives for the writer.

> Ladle the soup into four (or 4) bowls.
>
> Keep refrigerated for up to three (or 3) days.
>
> Spread out on two (or 2) baking sheets

TWO NUMBERS TOGETHER

When two numbers occur together in an ingredients list, there is a possibility of misreading. If figures are used for both, they tend to run together—"1 7-ounce can" is easily read as "17-ounce can."

There are two preferred ways to avoid this: use parentheses or change the wording. Do not spell out the first number because the otherwise orderly column of ingredients will be unsightly and askew. Do not spell out the second number because it will not be as clear and will create inconsistencies.

POOR: 1 3-pound chicken
POOR: One 3-pound chicken
POOR: 1 three-pound chicken

GOOD: 1 (3-pound) chicken
GOOD: 1 chicken, about 3 pounds

POOR: 2 20-ounce cans tomatoes
POOR: Two 20-ounce cans tomatoes
POOR: 2 twenty-ounce cans tomatoes

GOOD: 2 cans (20 ounces each) tomatoes
GOOD: 2 (20-ounce) cans tomatoes

When two figures occur together in recipe instructions, spell out the first one.

> Shape into loaves and place in two 9-inch loaf pans that have been thoroughly buttered.

You will need two 6-cup metal bowls.

An 8-ounce tin holds forty 1½-inch cookies.

Lightly oil two 1-pound coffee cans or three 1-pound vegetable or fruit cans.

WITH SERVINGS

Use figures for numbers of servings.

Makes 4 dozen cookies
Serves 6
Yield: 80 bite-size truffles
Makes 6 to 8 servings

Where two numbers occur together, spell out the first.

Yield: One 8 × 8-inch pan of rich fudge
Makes two 1-pound loaves

WITH DEGREES

Temperature degrees occurring in a recipe are set in figures. There are three ways to indicate the degrees (excluding centigrade) and all are acceptable, although we prefer the word degrees spelled out. This applies to oven temperatures, deep-fat thermometers, and candy thermometers.

SYMBOL	SPELLED OUT	WITH F
350°	350 degrees	400°F
		400 degrees F

If using the symbol and F, close up the space between them.

The use of F and C for Fahrenheit and centigrade is optional except in a work intended for countries other than the United States. In that case, it is best to give both temperatures.

Bake at 375°F/190°C

For conversion of Fahrenheit and centigrade temperatures, see page 192.

In general text, use the word "degree" rather than the symbol.

> Yeast begins to die when the liquid reaches 120 degrees.
>
> As long as the pork reaches an internal temperature of 140 degrees at the center, don't worry if it is slightly pink.
>
> In due course the dough will rise in a temperature as cool as 64 degrees.

Use the word "degree" when you are not referring to temperature readings.

> Give the dough a 90-degree turn.

IN LISTS

Figures can help to set off several points in a complicated sentence. It is best to enclose them in parentheses.

> There are a few ways to prevent the custard from curdling: (1) Cook it over a pot of simmering water rather than direct heat; (2) Keep a couple of tablespoons of chilled cream in the bowl into which you plan to strain the custard; (3) Set the bowl in a bed of ice cubes in order to cool the thickened custard completely.

IN INSTRUCTIONS

We prefer numbered steps in recipe instructions because the cook can refer to them easily and they highlight the beginning of a new step in the preparation. See page 31 about numbering steps.

DIMENSIONS

Use figures for compound measurements—length plus width and sometimes depth. "By" or lowercase "x" or the "multiplied by" sign (×) can be used to separate the numbers (capital "x" stands out unnecessarily). A good rule is to use "by" in headnotes and other narrative passages and " × " or "x," with space before and after, in recipe instructions.

NARRATIVE: 3 by 5 inches

RECIPES: 3 × 5 inches
3 x 5 inches

When the dimensions modify a noun, hyphenate only the last number.

an 8½ × 4½ × 2½-inch baking dish
a 10 by 5 by 3-inch loaf pan

FRACTIONS

Use figures for fractions in the list of ingredients. (Decimal points are never used in recipe writing.)

⅔ cup sifted cocoa
1½ teaspoons baking powder
¼ teaspoon baking soda
2½ cups all-purpose flour
12 tablespoons (1½ sticks) butter

Use figures for fractions in the instructions when referring to specific measurements.

Add the ½ cup confectioners' sugar, folding in very gently.

You may substitute 1½ tablespoons hot cream for the butter.

A beaten egg or ½ cup chopped onion sautéed in a little butter may be added before shaping the cakes.

Spell out fractions (both adjectives and nouns) used in a general sense in the instructions. (See also hyphens with numbers, page 97.)

Fill the pan two-thirds full

Reduce the sauce by one third

Stir one half the egg whites into the batter

In the manuscript, do not insert a hyphen between a numeral and a fraction, which often occurs with word processors. If such hyphens appear, the copy editor should remove them.

POOR: 1-½ cups sugar
GOOD: 1½ cups sugar

POOR: a 1-¾-quart casserole
GOOD: a 1¾-quart casserole

RANGES

When a range or choice of sizes is given in a compound adjective, there should be space following the first hyphen.

in an 8- or 10-inch skillet
a 12- to 14-inch pastry bag
an 18- to 20-pound turkey

When a temperature range is given, repeat the symbol if it is used.

Bake at 325° to 350° until brown, about 20 minutes.

WITH ABBREVIATIONS

Numbers used with abbreviations should be expressed in figures.

Spoon the pâte à choux into a pastry bag fitted with a plain No. 6 tip.

Lay the rabbit on its back with the hind legs away from you (see Fig. 1).

IN CROSS-REFERENCES

Always use figures for page numbers. (See also the discussion of cross-references on page 159.)

> My own sweet spice blend, given on page 333, includes a little true pepper.
>
> 1 cup béarnaise sauce (page 333)

When referring to chapters or parts of a book, use the form in which they originally appear.

> Consult Chapter 6 for how long to cook lamb.
>
> A spate of recipes for nonroasted birds will be found in Chapter Seven.
>
> For a discussion of stone milling, see Part I: History and Background.

IN GENERAL TEXT

Numbers in headnotes and other narrative passages, as opposed to those in the actual recipes, should be expressed in the standard house style of a publication. Lacking that, here is a brief summary of the forms used in most publishing houses.

Spell out numbers up to one hundred:

> One ounce of baker's yeast is ample for aerating up to four and one-half pounds of flour over two one-hour rising periods.
>
> On Christmas Eve in Provence it is customary to offer thirteen sweets as the dessert course.
>
> The eggs, only from ducks, are coated with a blend of lime, ashes, and salt and are left to stand for forty-five days.

Spell out round numbers from one to ninety-nine followed by hundred, thousand, million, etc.

> A fifteen-cubic-foot freezer will hold about five hundred pounds of food.
>
> Harvard beets were concocted in an English tavern called Harwood's more than three hundred years ago.
>
> Legend has it that sushi began two thousand years ago near Tokyo with an emperor who dined on fish that was just beginning to ferment.

Use figures for specific numbers over 100.

> When white sugar became available to the Kentucky Shakers, they recorded that 3,008 jars of peaches had been canned for market.
>
> Endive is cultivated by hand, as it has been for the past 125 years, on the flatlands that surround Brussels.

When small and large numbers appear in the same sentence, use figures for all when they refer to the same things.

> Vealers are grain-fed animals slaughtered at twelve weeks and weighing 150 to 200 pounds; calves are allowed to grow six months and weigh 250 to 300 pounds.
>
> The book consists of 196 pages, 50 of which are devoted to apple recipes.

Use figures for percentages.

> A medium potato contains about 100 calories, or 4 to 5 percent of the calories needed by the average adult in a day.
>
> Peanuts are 26 percent protein and 48 percent fat by weight.

A mixture of coarsely milled barley meal and 85 percent wheat meal makes delicious bread.

NUMBERS BEGINNING A SENTENCE

Never begin a sentence with a figure. If the figure is a year, it is best to recast the sentence.

POOR: 3 hours should be allowed for preparation.
GOOD: Three hours should be allowed for preparation.
GOOD: Allow 3 hours for preparation.

POOR: 1988 was a superb year for Beaujolais.
POOR: Nineteen eighty-eight was a superb year for Beaujolais.
GOOD: The 1988 Beaujolais was superb.
GOOD: The Beaujolais region produced superb vintages in 1988.

When two related numbers are used to open a sentence, spell out both of them.

Four or five 2-inch molds will be needed for this quantity.

Two to three cups will be plenty.

5

Capitalization

CAPITALIZATION, a seemingly noncontroversial issue in the population at large, can cause heated debate in food-writing circles. Food writers do not usually have strong feelings about the subject, but copy editors do.

The differences are between those who endorse an "up" style (a liberal use of capitals) and the advocates of a "down" style (few capitals).

The latter is favored by *The Chicago Manual of Style* and, less emphatically, by *Words into Type,* the two general stylebooks most often used in publishing. We also prefer an abstemious use of capitals—a down style.

In recipes and in the text that accompanies them, an up style is often favored to draw attention to other recipes and instructions in the article or book. But it is this very function of capitalization—one of formal emphasis—that can be intimidating and makes reading less smooth.

If a term used in a particular sense is capped once, however, it should be capped throughout the manuscript.

— In Titles —

GENERAL RULES

Capitalize the first letter of each word in a recipe title and subtitle, with the exception of articles *(a, an, the),* prepositions shorter than four letters *(at, by, for, in, of, off, on, to, up),* and coordinate conjunctions *(and, but, or, nor, for, yet, so).* The first and last words of a title should be capped regardless of the part of speech. The infinitive form is capitalized thus: *to Chop, to Sauté, to Microwave.*

Roast Haunch of Venison
Leek and Sausage Pie
Salmon Mousse in Aspic
Chicken Fricassee for a Crowd
A Chocolate Soufflé Worth Waiting For

Follow the same rules for titles in foreign languages, even though romance languages capitalize only the first word of a title, or the first word and the first noun.

Lasagne Frutti di Mare
Tarte aux Pommes
Ensalada de Tomate y Huevo
Rotkraut mit Speckäpfeln
Kreas me Kolokithia

PREPOSITIONS

Many publications capitalize prepositions of four or more letters.

DOWN STYLE	UP STYLE
Flank Steak with Herb Stuffing	Flank Steak With Herb Stuffing
Lamb Curry from Sumatra	Lamb Curry From Sumatra
All about Vinegar	All About Vinegar
Differences between Yeast and Baking Powder	Differences Between Yeast and Baking Powder

Those who prefer a down style will lowercase all prepositions, regardless of length, unless they are an inseparable part of the verb (see below) or occur at the beginning or end of a title.

Capitalize prepositions in a title when they are an inseparable part of the verb.

Cutting Up in the Kitchen
Hosing Down the Honey Extractor
Moving On to the Food Processor

COMPOUND WORDS

When compound words appear in a title, follow the up or down style used throughout the manuscript.

DOWN STYLE	UP STYLE
Red-cooked Duck	Red-Cooked Duck
Stir-fried Fish with Tree Ears	Stir-Fried Fish with Tree Ears
Old-fashioned Sugar Cookies	Old-Fashioned Sugar Cookies
Pan-fried Abalone	Pan-Fried Abalone
Slow-simmered Short Ribs	Slow-Simmered Short Ribs

AFTER CONNECTORS

If a title contains a hyphen or an en dash used as a connector between two or more nouns of equal value, capitalize all the nouns. The hyphen or dash in effect replaces the word *and.*

Strawberry-Rhubarb Pie
Sesame-Oatmeal Crisps
Chocolate Chip–Oatmeal Cookies
Calf's Brains in Mushroom-Cream Sauce

MARKING THE MANUSCRIPT

If the manuscript is typed with titles in all caps, the editor should indicate the correct capitalization in case the book designer or art director decides to use an uppercase and lowercase style. Do this by putting three lines under the letter that should be capped. Do not strike through the parts of words that should be lowercase because it may result in confusion on the part of the compositor.

POOR: PAN-FRIED BEEFSTEAKS ALLA CACCIATORA

GOOD: PAN-FRIED BEEFSTEAKS ALLA CACCIATORA

—*In Ingredients List*—

WITHOUT QUANTITIES

Use initial caps for ingredients not preceded by quantities. Otherwise the ingredient may look like a continuation of the line above, particularly if turnover lines are not deeply indented.

Salt and freshly ground
 pepper
Grated nutmeg
Oil for deep-frying
Pinch of thyme
Juice of 1 lemon
Freshly grated Parmesan
 cheese

WITHIN PARENTHESES

When an ingredient has a parenthetical instruction, lowercase the information in parentheses, even if it is a complete sentence.

1 cup chopped scallions (include both white and green parts)

1 duckling, steamed (see page 333)

2 cups chicken stock (canned broth works fine in this recipe)

WITH CROSS-REFERENCES

It's time to break with tradition in the matter of capitalization of the titles of recipes that appear elsewhere in the same manuscript. The purpose, in the days when it was too expensive to insert page numbers, was to make it easy for the reader to find the recipes in the index.

But that is no longer necessary when page references are included. Capitalization clutters the ingredients list, is intimidating, and grows even more confusing to the reader when main recipes are capitalized but such common ones as mayonnaise and chicken stock are not, although cross-references are given.

We recommend the following style:

1½ cups red pepper purée (page 333)
3 cups pecan rice (page 333)
Sour cream pastry (recipe follows)

If the author or editor insists on capitalizing cross-references in the ingredients list, they should be lowercased in the instructions.

INGREDIENTS LIST	INSTRUCTIONS
8 cups Duck Stock (page 333)	Stir 1 cup of the duck stock into the vegetables.
2 tablespoons diced rind of Moroccan Preserved Lemons (page 333)	Add the prunes and the preserved lemon rind.

—References to Other Parts— of the Book

The writer should capitalize parts of his own book when referring to them.

> Any good chewy, crusty bread will do, or make your own (see Index).
>
> As I said in the Introduction, I almost never serve hors d'oeuvres with drinks.
>
> See Chapter 1, "About the Kitchen," for further suggestions.

—General Rules—

PROPER NOUNS AND ADJECTIVES

Proper nouns and adjectives used in specialized meanings in recipe writing are often lowercased.

> brussels sprouts
> charlotte russe
> crepes suzette
> génoise
> mandarin orange
> napoleon

It is customary in English to capitalize proper adjectives used to describe the style in which a dish is cooked. Most foreign languages, however, do not, and the writer and editor can choose either style as long as it is consistent.

DOWN STYLE	UP STYLE
veal milanese	veal Milanese
eggplant alla siciliana	eggplant alla Siciliana
salade niçoise	salade Niçoise
boeuf bourguignonne	boeuf Bourguignonne

TRADE NAMES

Capitalize trade names, but do not use the symbol for a registered trademark, ® or ™, unless the material is for advertising or promotional materials for company products. The law does not require it and the capital letter is sufficient to indicate that it is a trade name.

See the Word List, Chapter 10, for some specific names.

GENUS AND SPECIES

Italicize the scientific names of plants and capitalize the genus, but lowercase the species.

> There is nothing like the first sprouts of *Asparagus officinalis* during the first days of spring.
>
> The edible wild mushroom *(Agaricus bisporus)* can be one of nature's delights.
>
> Broccoli *(Brassica oleracea italica)* is said to be particularly appealing to Geminis.

Lowercase a noun derived from the genus and set it in roman, not italic type.

> Of all the brassicas, broccoli is my favorite.
>
> Chives are the most delicately flavored members of the allium family.

GEOGRAPHICAL WORDS

Capitalize names derived from compass points when they are established as definite geographical sections.

> The South is justly famous for its fried chicken and mint juleps, its beaten biscuits and sweet potato pie.
>
> Tex-Mex cooking is an invention that began in the Southwest.

TEMPERATURES

Capitalize Fahrenheit when spelled out. Lowercase centigrade. Capitalize both when they are abbreviated (F and C). Celsius is the name of the Swede who invented the centigrade system and there is a growing movement to designate the system by his name. But centigrade is still more common in North America and thus preferred.

HOLIDAYS

Capitalize the names of holidays, holy days, and festivals.

> They were to be kept *para Navidad,* for Christmas.
>
> A favorite Passover breakfast treat, matzo brei is really a first cousin to French toast.
>
> I love New Year's Eve the way I love a warm blanket, a roaring fire, and an extra-dry martini.
>
> To me, Thanksgiving is one of the most sentimental of holidays—one in which you can, without apology, go back to the favorite foods of your childhood.

— *Wines and Liqueurs* —

This is one of the most confusing—and inconsistent—areas of capitalization. Dictionaries are of no help because they do not contain most of these terms. The easy way out is to capitalize all wines and lowercase the grapes from which they are made (unless the grape is named for a person, such as Maréchal Foch).

But since the trend is to a down style in general usage and in specialized language, we favor the five rules set forth by William Safire in his column "On Language: Wines Without Caps" in *The New York Times Magazine.*

We reprint them here, with the permission of *The Times.*

> Rule 1: When a wine is named for a place, and actually comes from that place, capitalize its name. Thus, for the wine from the Burgundy and Bordeaux regions of France, as well as bubbly from Champagne and brandy from Cognac—all real places—the first letter is uppercased.
>
> Rule 2: When a wine is named for a place but does not come from that place, do not capitalize. Thus, we have burgundy made in California, chablis from New York State. You like Chianti? Fine, capitalize if it's from somewhere near that place in Italy, but not if it's California chianti, or if it is Sicilian chianti.
>
> Rule 3: When a wine is named after a grape, do not capitalize—unless the grape is named after a place and the wine comes from that place. Now we're getting into deep water, or profound wine. Cabernet Sauvignon originated in Bordeaux, and if the wine comes from there, capitalize; *cabernet* is the name of the grape, not a city, and deserves no capital. Neither is pinot noir named after a town; its French name derives partially from "pine cone," which describes the shape of the grape cluster, and the wine's name is not capitalized. Wine carrying the name *tokay* is named after a grape that is named after a town in Hungary, so the only time to capitalize a tokay is when the wine comes from around that town in Hungary.
>
> Rule 4: If the wine is named after a place and comes from that place, but the name has changed slightly in transmission from place to wine, do not capitalize. Thus, the wine called *sherry* is never capitalized, even when it comes from Jerez, originally Xeres, in Spain. In the same way, forget about capitalizing *port,* because Oporto suffered a clip.

Rule 5: If the law calls for a certain spelling, for the purpose of identifying the point of origin to the consumer, obey the law. I generally resist language-by-fiat, but am willing to go along on a ukase-by-ukase basis with those legislative requirements limiting the name Cognac to the brandy distilled from wine produced in that area, and calling all other brandy merely brandy, or grappa, or marc, or weinbrand. Rory Callahan, spokesman for the Wine Institute, representing California wines, points out that the American version of French Sauternes must not be spelled with the final s, to distinguish it from the American product: it's American sauterne.

—*Miscellaneous*—

Names of cheeses vary widely in capitalization in dictionaries. Apply the same rules to cheese as to wine (see above).

See the "Word List," Chapter 10, for some specific fruits and vegetables that are capitalized.

See "Indexing," Chapter 6, for capitalization in that specific area.

See page 93 for capitalization after a colon.

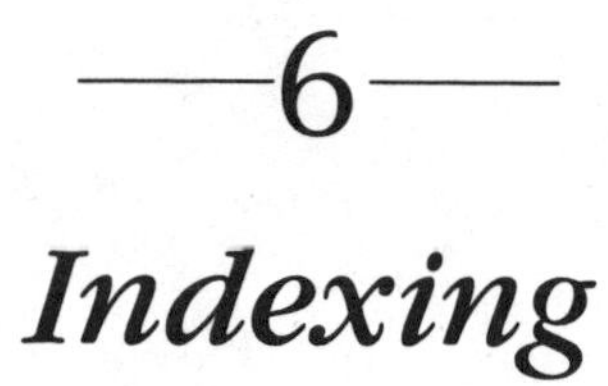

6
Indexing

IN A COOKBOOK, an index is second in importance only to the quality of the recipes. Without a good index, the recipes the reader is looking for cannot be located. Unfortunately, this essential element cannot be compiled until the book is in page proof, and therefore it almost always must be prepared under the pressure of time. Thus, there isn't much time to repair an index not to the author's liking.

There are some things, however, that an author can think about ahead to ensure a good job:

- Recipe titles, and whether they will be difficult to categorize.
- Whether the variations are to be indexed. If they are, make sure the variations have real titles, not just Variation.
- The amount of space allotted for the index is usually out of the author's control. But if he prefers a detailed index, he should make his wishes known early so that the designer will take this into consideration.

Indexing any book, particularly a cookbook, is not an exact science. It is very personal and there are widely differing views on what constitutes a good index. Some prefer an extremely detailed index, with almost every word in a recipe title listed. Others prefer to index only the essential elements.

Whichever kind is chosen, the index must be clear. It must be easy to read, categories must be easy to find, and it must be in acceptable

English form. This requires thought and knowledge on the part of the indexer, and since in most book publishing contracts the author pays for the index, he should demand the best. Indexers are almost always free-lancers and do not work for only one publishing house. Ideally, an author should be able to find an index he likes in another book by his own publisher and ask for the free-lancer responsible for it to compile the index for his book.

Authors are not objective enough to index their own work. It takes professional skill to know what is important and what is peripheral, and to organize an index in the most useful manner for readers.

TYPOGRAPHICAL CLARITY

Two elements make a cookbook index easy to read and to find things in:

Continued lines when appropriate at the top of each column:

Chicken, *continued*

Subentries indented, rather than run in, with no more than two levels of indentation

POOR	GOOD

Soup, game, with pears,
  213; gazpacho, 266;
  potato, leek, and
  ham, 201
	Soup
	  game, with pears, 213
	  gazpacho, 266
	  potato, leek, and ham, 201

POOR	GOOD

Chicken
  liver(s)
    pâté
      and ham, 22
      and mushroom, 23
    sauce for tongue, 457
	Chicken
	  liver(s)
	    pâté: ham, 22; mushroom, 23
	    sauce for tongue, 457

CAPITALIZATION

There are four styles of capitalization in indexing. All are acceptable, but some have drawbacks with recipe titles. We recommend a Modified Lowercase style (Fig. 3) both for clarity and for ease in finding things.

Formal indexes use an extreme uppercase style. All main entries are capitalized and all subentries that are recipe titles, or fragments of recipe titles, are capitalized. (See Fig. 1, page 136.)

Modified Uppercase-style indexes are those in which all exact recipe titles are capitalized. Main entries are lowercase except for the usual proper nouns, and descriptive recipe names, as opposed to exact titles, are lowercase. (See Fig. 2.)

Modified Lowercase is a style in which all main entries are capitalized (initial cap only, meaning that only the first word is capitalized, even for exact recipe titles) and all subentries, whether they are recipe titles or not, are lowercase. (See Fig. 3.)

Informal indexes employ an extreme lowercase style. All main entries, subentries, and recipe titles are lowercase; only proper names are capitalized. (See Fig. 4.)

Examples of the four styles appear on the two pages immediately following.

Fig. 1.
FORMAL INDEX

Pain d'Épice, 220
Pan Bagna, 23
Pancakes
  Buckwheat, 61
  Buttermilk, 62
  Scallion, 136
Pancetta
  about, 6
  and Escarole Frittata, 32
  Polenta con, 19
Pandowdy, Apple, 316
Panettone, 243
Pan-Fried Fish, 187
Papaya
  with Prosciutto, 28
  raw, as dessert, 363
  Salsa, 26
  Tart with Macadamia Nuts, 364
Pappa al Pomodoro, 87
Paprika
  Cabbage Filling, 113
  Sauce, Lobster in, 181
  in Tandoori, 163
  types of, 8
Paris-Brest, 219
Parsnip(s)
  Basic Method for Cooking, 118
  in Bundles with Bean Curd, 119
  Chowder, 86
Pasta
  Agnolotti di Zucca, 17
  Bow-Tie, and Mushrooms, 16
  Primavera, 15
  alla Puttanesca, 16
Pâte à Choux, 218
  Cheese Puffs, 22
  Paris-Brest, 219
  Sucré, 220
Paupiettes de Veau, 195

Fig. 2.
MODIFIED
UPPERCASE-STYLE INDEX

Pain d'Épice, 220
Pan Bagna, 23
pancakes
  Buckwheat Pancakes, 61
  Buttermilk Pancakes, 62
  Scallion Pancakes, 136
pancetta
  about, 6
  Pancetta and Escarole Fritters, 32
  Polenta con Pancetta, 19
pandowdy, apple, 316
Panettone, 243
Pan-Fried Fish, 187
Papaya
  Papaya with Prosciutto, 28
  Papaya Salsa, 26
  Papaya Tart with Macadamia Nuts, 364
  raw, as dessert, 363
Pappa al Pomodoro, 87
paprika
  Paprika Cabbage Filling, 113
  sauce, lobster in, 181
  in tandoori, 163
  types of, 8
Paris-Brest, 219
parsnip(s)
  basic method for cooking, 118
  Parsnips in Bundles with Bean Curd, 11
  Parsnip Chowder, 86
pasta
  Agnolotti di Zucca, 17
  Bow-Tie Pasta and Mushrooms, 16
  Pasta Primavera, 15
  Pasta alla Puttanesca, 16
Pâte à Choux, 218
  Cheese Puffs, 22
  Paris-Brest, 219
  Pâte à Choux Sucré, 220
Paupiettes de Veau, 195

Fig. 3.
MODIFIED
LOWERCASE-STYLE INDEX

- Pain d'épice, 220
- Pan bagna, 23
- Pancakes
  - buckwheat, 61
  - buttermilk, 62
  - scallion, 136
- Pancetta
  - about, 6
  - and escarole frittata, 32
  - polenta con, 19
- Pandowdy, apple, 316
- Panettone, 243
- Pan-fried fish, 187
- Papaya
  - with prosciutto, 28
  - raw, as dessert, 363
  - salsa, 26
  - tart with macadamia nuts, 364
- Pappa al pomodoro, 87
- Paprika
  - cabbage filling, 113
  - sauce, lobster in, 181
  - in tandoori, 163
  - types of, 8
- Paris-brest, 219
- Parsnip(s)
  - basic method for cooking, 118
  - in bundles with bean curd, 119
  - chowder, 86
- Pasta
  - agnolotti di zucca, 17
  - alla puttanesca, 16
  - bow-tie, and mushrooms, 16
  - primavera, 15
- Pâte à choux, 218
  - cheese puffs, 22
  - Paris-brest, 219
  - sucré, 220
- Paupiettes de veau, 195

Fig. 4.
INFORMAL INDEX

- pain d'épice, 220
- pan bagna, 23
- pancakes
  - buckwheat, 61
  - buttermilk, 62
  - scallion, 136
- pancetta
  - about, 6
  - and escarole frittata, 32
  - polenta con, 19
- pandowdy, apple, 316
- panettone, 243
- pan-fried fish, 187
- papaya
  - with prosciutto, 28
  - raw, as dessert, 363
  - salsa, 26
  - tart with macadamia nuts, 364
- pappa al pomodoro, 87
- paprika
  - cabbage filling, 113
  - sauce, lobster in, 181
  - in tandoori, 163
  - types of, 8
- Paris-brest, 219
- parsnips
  - basic method for cooking, 118
  - in bundles with bean curd, 119
  - chowder, 86
- pasta
  - agnolotti di zucca, 17
  - alla puttanesca, 16
  - bow-tie, and mushrooms, 16
  - primavera, 15
- pâte à choux, 218
  - cheese puffs, 22
  - Paris-brest, 219
  - sucré, 220
- paupiettes de veau, 195

ALPHABETIZING

Use the system called letter-by-letter, or dictionary style, which treats the whole entry as one word up to the first comma, without regard to spaces between words. Thus, sweetbreads would come before sweet potatoes. In word-by-word, or phone-book style, all the entries starting with sweet would be entered before solid compounds whose first syllable is sweet.

It is easier for the reader to find what he's looking for when the index is alphabetized letter by letter.

WORD BY WORD (NOT RECOMMENDED)	LETTER BY LETTER (RECOMMENDED)
Sweet butter	Sweet-and-sour
Sweet cream	Sweetbreads
Sweet potato	Sweet butter
Sweet-and-sour	Sweet cream
Sweetbreads	Sweetmeats
Sweetmeats	Sweet potato
Sweetsop	Sweetsop

INCLUSIVE NUMBERS

The reader needs to know only the page on which the recipe begins, even if it covers two or more pages. Using inclusive numbers (323–25) takes up valuable space without adding to the cook's knowledge.

When textual information is being indexed, however, inclusive numbers are helpful. Which system of numbering to use usually depends on the style of the publishing house, but the following is the most commonly used format.

For the higher number, the last two digits only:
Baklava, 323–25

Exception: numbers 100–109, 200–209, etc., which are usually given in full:
100–103, 201–207, 306–308

MAIN ENTRIES

Some authors prefer to have every complete recipe title listed in the index. Few cookbook users, however, are going to look up something under *Easy* or *Hot* or *Fresh* or *Cream of.* And the purpose of an index should be to make it easy to find things.

A main entry should be a noun, or a noun phrase. Adjectives such as cold, hot, puréed, braised, boiled, buttered, fresh, sautéed, should not be main entries in an index, that is with subentries beneath them. In fact, most adjectives should not be indexed at all except in inverted form. There are, of course, exceptions.

If the author is emphasizing cooking methods or regional dishes, adjectives can be made into noun phrases and have subentries beneath.

COLD BROCCOLI SOUP

Index under Broccoli and under Soup. If the author wants a category called Cold soups, or Cold dishes, it can also be listed under that main entry.

STUFFED PEPPERS

Index under Peppers. If the author wants a category called Stuffed vegetables, it can also be listed under that main entry.

CANTONESE APPLE SLICES

Index under Apples. If the author wants a category called Cantonese dishes, it can also be listed under that main entry.

FRESH FRUIT WITH SABAYON

Index under Fruit and under Sabayon, but not under Fresh.

PIQUANT RELISH

Index only under Relish.

Exceptions: When the adjective is an integral part of the recipe title, the complete title should be listed.

Black bottom pie	Brown Betty
Clarified butter	Fried rice
Hard sauce	Hot-and-sour soup
Hot fudge sauce	Indian pudding
Parker House rolls	Red flannel hash
Scalloped potatoes	Soft-shell crabs
Sun-dried tomatoes	Wiener schnitzel

INVERSIONS

In both main entries and subentries, bring the main word to the key position.

Soup
  broccoli, cream of (not cream of broccoli)

Cabbage, red and white, sautéed (not sautéed red and white)

Tart
  almond, Lindsey's (not Lindsey's almond)
  mushroom, excellent (not excellent mushroom)

When the cooking method is the first word of the recipe title, invert the noun and the adjective.

Onions, braised
Eggplant, broiled
Parsnips, sautéed
Potatoes, puréed
Scallions, boiled

MULTIPLE ENTRIES

Listing a recipe under more than one main entry is where personal preference comes into play. The following examples would be indexed similarly by almost everyone. Each underlined word is a main entry.

Cranberry and kumquat conserve
Almond Torte (also under Cake)
Escabeche of Fish
Grapefruit Sorbet
Beet and Cabbage Soup

The problem arises with secondary parts of the recipe.

Game Soup with Pears

No one is going to look under pears to see what to do with them and come up with game soup. List only under Game and Soup.

Catfish with Sesame Seeds

This should be indexed under Sesame Seeds only if the book is a specialized one on nuts and seeds.

Hot Broccoli Salad with Caper Sauce

Unless the caper sauce is a subsidiary recipe with its own title, index only under Broccoli and Salad.

Chayotes Stuffed with Cheese

This may also be indexed under Squash and Vegetables, and possibly Stuffed vegetables, but it should not be listed under Cheese.

Sauerkraut Cooked in Wine

List also under Cabbage, but not under Wine.

Lima Beans in Cream Sauce

This should also be listed under Beans, but not under Cream or Sauce.

Cucumbers in Sour Cream with Dill

This should be listed under Dill only if the book is mainly about herbs. Do not list under sour cream.

Bluefish Seviche with Red Onion and Hot Pepper Flakes

Index only under main title. Do not index a garnish or seasoning.

Ham Roulade with Mustard–Sour Cream Sauce

When a subsidiary recipe is part of the title, index the secondary part as well as the main title.

When an ingredient is a distinctive or essential part of the dish, it is desirable to list the secondary element as well as the first. Each underlined term is a main entry.

Chick-pea Salad with Tahini
Maize Custards with Mushroom Purée
Puff Pastries with Blood Oranges

A good cookbook indexer must possess a certain amount of culinary knowledge in order to decide on multiple entries.

Duxelles—list also under Mushrooms
Coleslaw—list also under Cabbage and Salads
Guacamole—list also under Avocado
Pain d'Épice—list also under Breads and Cakes
Sashimi—list also under Fish
Bûche de Noël—list also under Cakes
Oeufs à la Neige—list also under Meringue
Succotash—list also under Lima beans and Corn
Poor Man's Caviar—list also under Eggplant

When a recipe title has two elements of almost equal value, the elements should be inverted when the title is cross-indexed. For the listing under the general category, use the order in which it was given in the recipe title.

Green bean and mushroom salad
Mushroom and green bean salad
Salad
  green bean and mushroom

Rhubarb and strawberry pie
Strawberry and rhubarb pie
Pie
  rhubarb and strawberry

Jerusalem artichoke and cranberry fritters
Cranberry and Jerusalem artichoke fritters
Fritters
  Jerusalem artichoke and cranberry

CROSS-REFERENCES

Use a cross-reference to direct an index user to another entry that is complete with subentries and page numbers.

Chowder, *see* Soups
Gigot, *see* Lamb

Use a *see also* reference to guide the reader to additional information.

Vegetable(s)
  creamed, 123
  purchasing and storing, 234
  soup, 116
  see also specific vegetables

Do not use a cross-reference for a single recipe that is indexed in more than one place. Give the page number in each instance.

All-day beef stew, 123
Beef stew, 123
Stew, beef, 123

PROPER NAMES

As discussed in Chapter 1, attribution in recipe titles should be done sparingly, but some writers feel that it is important to acknowledge their contributors in this way. If the complete name does appear in the title, index it in one of two ways:

TOM ISBEL'S PARSLEY SALAD

Isbel, Tom: parsley salad, 80
Isbel, Tom, 80

In both cases, the other listings should be:

Parsley salad, Tom Isbel's, 90
Salad
  parsley, Tom Isbel's, 80

If only the first name is used, index under the name.

Billy's coleslaw, 90
Coleslaw, Billy's, 90

FOREIGN TITLES

If a cookbook has foreign recipe titles throughout, there are several ways to handle these in an index.

The foreign titles can be listed in a separate index. This can be effective because the reader does not have to make constant mental translation shifts. It can be troublesome, however, when the reader starts with the wrong index.

Foreign titles that are entries in their own right, not just literal translations, can be listed in roman type. Foreign categories can be listed by noun or phrase followed by *see* or *see also* with a reference to the English category. This simplified method (see Fig. 5) makes a handsome index, one that is easy to use, and the one we recommend.

The foreign titles can be listed in the overall index and italicized. Mixed indexes can be choppy looking, however, and when an index contains both italicized entries and capitalized recipe titles (see Fig. 6), it can be typographically chaotic.

Fig. 5
INDEX WITH FOREIGN TITLES IN ROMAN

- Pain d'épice, 220
- Pan bagna, 23
- Pancakes
  - buckwheat, 61
  - buttermilk, 62
  - scallion, 136
- Pancetta
  - about, 6
  - and escarole frittata, 32
  - polenta con, 19
- Pandowdy, apple, 316
- Panettone, 243
- Pan-fried fish, 187
- Papaya
  - with prosciutto, 28
  - raw, as dessert, 363
  - salsa, 26
  - tart with macadamia nuts, 364
- Pappa al pomodoro, 87
- Paprika
  - cabbage filling, 113
  - sauce, lobster in, 181
  - in tandoori, 163
  - types of, 8
- Paris-brest, 219
- Parsnip(s)
  - basic method for cooking, 118
  - in bundles with bean curd, 119
  - chowder, 86
- Pasta
  - agnolotti di zucca, 17
  - bow-tie, and mushrooms, 16

Fig. 6.
MIXED-STYLE INDEX

- *Pain d'Épice,* 220
- *Pan Bagna,* 23
- Pancakes
  - Buckwheat, 61
  - Buttermilk, 62
  - Scallion, 136
- *Pancetta*
  - about, 6
  - and Escarole Frittata, 32
  - *Polenta con,* 19
- Pandowdy, Apple, 316
- *Panettone,* 243
- Pan-Fried Fish, 187
- Papaya
  - with Prosciutto, 28
  - raw, as dessert, 363
  - Salsa, 26
  - Tart with Macadamia Nuts, 364
- *Pappa al Pomodoro,* 87
- Paprika
  - Cabbage Filling, 113
  - Sauce, Lobster in, 181
  - in *Tandoori,* 163
  - types of, 8
- *Paris-Brest,* 219
- Parsnip(s)
  - Basic Method for Cooking, 118
  - in Bundles with Bean Curd, 119
  - Chowder, 86
- Pasta
  - *Agnolotti di Zucca,* 17
  - Bow-Tie, and Mushrooms, 16

If space permits, it is helpful to include the foreign name of the recipe along with the English version. But do not do this when the foreign title is merely a translation of the English.

POOR: Chicken and wild rice casserole (timbale de volaille et riz sauvage), 230
Lamb, leg of, English style (gigot d'agneau à l'anglaise), 242

GOOD: Meringue with tropical fruits (Pavlova), 343
Sand cookies (polvorones), 63
Tripe soup (menudo), 16

GENERAL INDEX VS. RECIPE INDEX

Many cooks have experienced the frustration of looking for a recipe that has been listed in the index only to find a discussion of—and not a recipe for—the dish in question. When a dish is discussed in a cookbook but no recipe is given for it, it should appear in the index with suitable warning. This can be handled in various ways.

- Qualify the entry with the words "discussion of" or "discussed," or some other device.

  Truite au bleu, discussed, 123
  Haggis, role of in Burns supper, 234
  Tuna fish casserole, as Friday-night institution, 345

- Use boldface page numbers for actual recipes, with a line of explanation at the beginning of the index, directly under the title. Italic type is not recommended because italic numbers are not readily distinguishable from roman.

INDEX
(Page numbers in **boldface** refer to recipes)

In books about food and cooking that contain only an incidental number of recipes, the recipes should be clearly indicated in the index.

Truffles, 23, 45, 67
  method of harvesting, 24–25
  types of, 46–48
  with scrambled eggs (recipe), 68

—7—

Preparation of the Manuscript

CAREFUL PREPARATION of a manuscript is an important step in assuring an error-free article, pamphlet, or book. Most of the suggestions in this chapter refer to manuscripts to be submitted to book publishers, but some apply to articles for newspapers, periodicals, or pamphlets.

In all cases, the steps involve the author, editor, copy editor, production editor, and designer or art director.

—*The Typescript*—

It is the author's responsibility to provide legible copy prepared according to certain standards—whether for an article for a newspaper or periodical, or for a collection of recipes for a pamphlet or book.

- Double space all text and all parts of a recipe, including the ingredients list.
- Margins should be at least one and one-half inches top and bottom and on both sides of the page.
- Type the headings, chapter titles, and recipe titles upper and lower case. The art director or designer will decide what will be in all caps.
- If using a word processor or typewriter with changeable type faces, don't italicize or boldface words. If italics are desired, underline the word; for boldface, use a wavy line.

- Number each page in the top right-hand corner.
- No more than one recipe should appear on a page, because the recipes may be rearranged during the course of editing.
- When a recipe takes up more than one page, the second and following pages should carry an identifying line—for example: Baked custard, page 2.
- Type an insert on a separate page and mark it clearly. Place it following the page where it is to be inserted and number it 52a, for example. Do not type or write inserts in the margins or on the back of the page.
- Submit an original and one copy of the manuscript on good-quality paper to the publisher.

— *Arrangement of Chapters* —

Cookbooks fall into two major categories: general and specialty. The selection and arrangement of material are somewhat different in the two types.

The most logical way to organize a general cookbook—and many specialized ones—is chronologically through the order of a meal, from appetizers to desserts.

Within the chapters, recipes can proceed from simple to complex, from cold to hot. Vegetables are traditionally arranged in alphabetical order, as are fish and seafood. Appetizers can range from cold to hot, or be organized by type—canapés, pâtés, dips, etc.

Kinds of meat should be kept together, as should types of poultry. Within these categories, recipes should be arranged by cuts of meat or poultry, or by method of preparation.

Pasta is frequently arranged by type (linguine, fusilli, etc.), but a more helpful order is by kind of sauce or preparation because the types of pasta are often interchangeable.

Desserts fall naturally into categories—pies, cakes, cookies, fruit, etc.

In specialty cookbooks that do not lend themselves to chronological arrangement, the order will be dictated by the nature of the specialization. In an herb and spice cookbook, for example, chapters are usually arranged alphabetically by the name of the herb or spice; in a bread book, they can be conveniently arranged by type (white, bran, whole wheat, sourdough, rye) or by category (yeast breads, quick breads, festive breads, rolls). It is a good idea to examine other books on the subject before making a final decision.

There is often a strong temptation to create a catchall heading for recipes that don't seem to fit anywhere else. A chapter entitled "Luncheon and Supper Dishes" can become a little graveyard in which are buried the tuna casserole and creamed chipped beef of yesteryear—along with some very good recipes that would be better noticed under a general category like "Fish" or "Meat." The author can be imaginative, if necessary, to fit recipes into specific categories—such chapter headings as "Accompaniments," "Side Dishes," and "Cooking on the Grill" are just a few.

SPECIAL INFORMATION

General cookbooks usually contain a variety of information that is placed either in the front of the book or in the back, just before the index—suggested menus, nutrition information, calorie charts, etc.

In specialty cookbooks, a statement of purpose and special information on the subject are placed in the beginning of the book because they are considered important enough to be read by the cook before he embarks on the recipes. This preliminary material may include chapters on ingredients and procedures, utensils, techniques, health information (if the recipes are for specialized diets), wines of a particular region, etc.

In both types of cookbooks, mail-order sources, bibliography, metric conversion tables, and, of course, the index, are placed in the back of the book.

Large specialty cookbooks are sometimes divided into units that are unrelated to food categories (by holidays, for example). In these cases, a list of recipes by category is a useful device in the front of the book; it should be positioned to follow the contents page.

— Order of Front Matter —

Front matter, the publishing term for the preliminary pages of a book, marches in an order long established by tradition, with minor deviations according to the practice of individual publishers. Here is an outline of the appropriate sequence of elements, not all of which will appear in every book.

Half title (only the title of the book, standing alone on the page)
Card page (list of author's previous books)
List of contributors
Title page
Copyright page, with legal acknowledgments
Dedication
Epigraph
Contents
List of illustrations
List of recipes by category
Acknowledgments
Foreword or introduction by someone other than the author
Author's preface, which can include personal acknowledgments
How to use the book
Second half title, if any, to indicate end of front matter

The author's introduction, setting the geographic, ethnic, or historic scene for the book, is usually the beginning of the text proper.

— *Contents Page* —

It is the author's responsibility to provide a table of contents with the completed manuscript. Its heading should be simply "Contents."

It should give an overall view of the structure of the work, enabling the reader to grasp the scope and nature of the material at a glance. For the author, the contents is an outline, organizing his material logically into units. And, of course, it lists page numbers for the convenience of the user, although it is by no means a substitute for the index.

Major elements of the front matter (preface, acknowledgments, foreword by someone other than the author) and all the back matter (mail-order sources, bibliography, index) should always be included in the contents.

Chapter titles—and their numbers if they are to be used—may be followed by major categories of each chapter, with or without their page numbers. Part titles are customarily entered in the contents, but the page numbers are omitted.

Many serious cookbooks contain a complete contents page, which lists chronologically not only part and chapter titles, but also all the main recipes in each chapter. This can be of interest to the bookstore browser and the researcher, but it is of little additional use to the cook. And for a publisher trying to keep costs down, it can be an extravagance. If a choice is to be made between a complete table of contents in the front of the book and a well-prepared index at the back, there should be no question about which should be sacrificed: a good index is far more useful and important.

— *Chapter-Contents Page* —

A chapter-contents page is a listing of all the main recipes contained in a chapter and is often printed on the back of a right-hand page occupied only by the chapter title. (In this book, chapter-contents listings begin under the chapter titles and continue on the back of the page where necessary.)

The chapter-contents page lists recipes in the order in which they are printed, but does not necessarily show the page numbers.

Such a complete listing is not mandatory in a cookbook (and sometimes is not feasible for space reasons or for cost), but it is a useful embellishment and can be a great convenience to the cook. Author and editor may need to confer on whether to include this form of presentation. If so, the author should include copy for it in the submitted manuscript. It can thus be designed as part of the book's basic format and space allowance made for it.

—Listing of Recipes by Category—

Specialty cookbooks that are organized around a theme often scatter recipes throughout the text, instead of in the orderly progression found in general cookbooks. The recipes may be organized by season, by method of cooking, by occasion, by region, and so on. This makes it difficult for the browser who wants to see quickly what kinds of recipes are included.

For such cookbooks, a front-matter listing of recipes by category is extremely useful. It should follow the contents page or the list of illustrations, and may be set in smaller type than the contents and appear in multiple-column format so as to take up as little space as possible. Its heading should be "Recipes by Category." Categories can include such subheadings as Appetizers, Soups, Cheese and Egg Dishes, Pasta, and so on. The listing does not include page numbers, so a line under the main heading should read: Consult the Index for page numbers.

— *List of Illustrations* —

A formal list of illustrations adds an elegant touch to a cookbook, and its use is recommended if space permits. This is particularly so when the illustrations are instructional rather than merely decorative. The author may supply such a list along with the manuscript, but it is usually prepared by the production editor. Its heading should be simply "Illustrations," set in the same type size as the contents heading.

The list of illustrations is an extension of the contents page and should be placed on the page immediately following. If it is considerably longer than the table of contents, it may be set in smaller type.

When more than one type of illustration appears in the book, it is customary, but not mandatory, to list them under separate headings: "Techniques," "Color Plates," "Drawings," etc.

Because placement of illustrations is determined when galley proofs are dummied, copy for the illustrations list is prepared after page numbering. The list should consist of short titles (not the entire caption) followed by the page number.

— *Headings* —

PARTS OR SECTIONS

A part or section is a major division of a book in which chapters are grouped logically. Not all books are divided into parts, and those that are may contain only two or three. The part title appears in a book on a separate page preceding the chapters it covers.

CHAPTERS

The chapters are the main divisions of a book. Chapters are titled and often numbered, although numbers are not necessary. Chapter titles should be relatively short and reasonably informative about what the chapter contains.

SUBHEADINGS

Cookbooks are studded with subheadings of many levels: the recipe title, the subsidiary recipe title, the variation, the yield line (or number of servings), and often a small heading in the ingredients list ("The garnish"). The author should handle these heads consistently in the manuscript—using placement and underlining to indicate his intentions—so that whoever keys the headings for the typesetter has a good idea of the weight to be assigned to them.

Fig. 7
TREATMENT OF HEADINGS

Headings	*Manuscript Treatment*	*Key Letters*
Part number and title:	Typed alone on its own page	PN, PT
Chapter number and title:	Type the number, if used, and title at least three inches down from the top of the page (a measurement called sinkage)	CN, CT
Major text head:	Centered and underlined	A
Minor text subhead:	Centered	B
Recipe title:	Centered	R or R-1
Subsidiary recipe title:	Flush left (starting at left margin with no indentation)	SR or R-2
Variation:	Type the word *Variation* at the beginning of the paragraph, underlined, and followed by a period	V or R-3
Ingredients subhead:	Flush left or centered over the column and underlined	C or R-4
Yield:	Flush left, placed at the beginning or end of the recipe. It should be typed alone on its own line	Y
Note:	Type the word *Note* at the beginning of the paragraph, underlined, and followed by a period	N

The food writer does not have to be concerned with final keying of the manuscript for the designer, which will be taken care of by the copy editor, the production editor, or the editor. Keying—by letter or letter plus number—gives the designer a guide as to how much weight each heading is to carry. It is then the designer's responsibility to indicate which typeface and size go with each letter, and this in turn directs the compositor in setting the manuscript.

Fig. 7 shows a suggested form for the food writer to use when setting up his manuscript, and a suggested list of key letters for the copy editor to use, based on their use in various publishing houses. Not all the headings will be appropriate, of course.

— *Cross-References* —

The cross-reference is a device used to refer the reader to a recipe or relevant procedure elsewhere in the text. It is a useful way to avoid repetition and to save space, but it should not be overused. Here is a hypothetical example of the worst abuse of cross-referencing:

CHOCOLATE PIE

Piecrust for a single-crust pie (page 333)
Chocolate pudding (page 333)
2 cups sweetened whipped cream (page 333)

Bake and cool the piecrust. Make the pudding and allow to cool. Shortly before serving, pour the pudding into the crust and top with the whipped cream.

Needless to say, the cook would be exasperated at having to search through the book for every procedure in this recipe. The ideal way to write a recipe for chocolate pie would be to include the complete ingredients and procedures on the same page, with the exception, perhaps, of the piecrust.

ADDING CROSS-REFERENCES IN THE MANUSCRIPT

It is the author's responsibility to indicate cross-referencing in a cookbook manuscript. Do this with "see page 000" or "see page ???" Do not type in the actual manuscript page number or it will almost certainly appear in the finished book.

It is helpful to have the author mark the correct manuscript page for a cross-reference in the margin and circle it. Otherwise, the copy editor should do this with the marginal notation "x-ref" and the manuscript page number, both circled. The copy editor can also instruct the typesetter to set solid slugs (■■■) for cross-references throughout. These large black signals leap quickly to the eye and thus help to avoid the embarrassment of an overlooked "see page 000" ending up in a finished book.

"SEE INDEX" VS. "SEE PAGE 333"

In present-day cookbooks it is inexcusable to omit the page number in a cross-reference and substitute "see Index" or "see recipe." This practice was perhaps born out of a Depression-era desire to avoid additional typesetting charges. It is false economy indeed in consideration of the ill will it can build for the book.

As we go to press, the approximate cost of resetting for a cross-reference is $2.00—a modest sum even when multiplied by 100 or more. It should be considered a normal part of the cookbook production process and not an author's alteration to be charged against royalties. A wise cookbook author will see that this is written into the contract.

SUPPLYING PAGE NUMBERS IN PROOFS

Once the final pagination of the book has been determined, the editor or production editor will supply page numbers for cross-references. These should be included in galley corrections so that the numbers can be verified in the next stage of proof; therefore, this work should be done as soon as the dummy (see page 167) is finished and approved.

Working directly on a photocopy of the dummy is infinitely preferable to working from a simple listing of which recipes fall on which pages. The dummy will be set up in double-page spreads so that facing pages will be immediately apparent.

The supplying of page numbers should be done intelligently rather than mechanically. There are often instances when "see opposite page" or "see instructions above" or "see illustrations on next two pages" is more appropriate than a simple page number. It is particularly important to avoid cross-referring to the same page the original recipe appears on—and yet this blunder can often be seen in otherwise well-produced books.

—*Adapting Recipes and Obtaining Permission to Reprint*—

Since many of the recipes that end up in published cookbooks are obtained from files that have accumulated over the years—from typed handouts in cooking classes, from ancient clippings, from friends' notes—the manuscript may well contain instances of unwitting plagiarism.

To avoid this, the author should make absolutely sure the recipe is in his own words, because it is the choice and arrangement of words that the copyright holder can lay claim to. (Recipe titles may not be copyrighted.) The best way to do this is to put the recipe through the typewriter again—changing the order of ingredients, adapting the recipe for larger or smaller quantities, reworking the language and writing style.

This is recommended only for a recipe whose source is honestly unknown. Where possible, give credit to the originator, preferably in a headnote (see page 14).

If the author wishes to reprint a recipe still in copyright, he will have to obtain permission to do so. This also holds true for substantial excerpts of prose, all verse and song lyrics, plus illustrations, maps, charts, or tables borrowed from sources protected by copyright.

Permission must be obtained in writing from the original publisher—oral permission from the author is not enough. Fig. 8 shows a sample permission request letter.

Fig. 8
SAMPLE PERMISSION REQUEST

Emma Jacob
Permissions Editor
Subsidiary Rights Department
Arachnid Publishers

Dear Editor:

For a book tentatively entitled ______________________________,
by _____________, to be published by ____________________
in July 1999, I would like your permission to reprint the following (copy attached):

> Rosie's Streusel Topping, page 333 of
> *JUST PLAIN DESSERTS* by Leslee Lynne,
> Arachnid Publishers, 1991

The book will be published as a trade paperback with a planned first printing of 20,000 and a tentative price of $15.

I would like permission for the U.S., Canada, Philippine Islands and the open market. *Please specify your exact credit and copyright line, plus fee if any.* If you do not control the rights, please tell me to whom I should write. You can call me direct at the phone number below; I will follow up this letter with a phone call if necessary.

Thank you for your prompt attention to this request.

—8—

Format and Typography

THE COOKBOOK EDITOR AND WRITER should know something about the various processes a manuscript goes through in its metamorphosis to a printed book. They should be aware of the potential problems that face the designer, typesetter, and indexer. And they should respect the professionalism that goes into book production, just as the designer, typesetter, and indexer should respect the editor's and writer's crafts.

The computer made possible significant changes in the publishing process. Small publishers and type houses have long since taken advantage of its possibilities in setting type. Now even larger commercial book publishers are beginning to experiment with what is called desktop publishing, a process by which copy can be written, edited, designed, and typeset all on the same machine.

Computer programs that combine a standard cookbook design format with programmed page makeup are used successfully by specialty publishers. These programs—usually geared to amateur fund-raising groups—can turn out a remarkably low-priced product in a short time. They proceed directly from manuscript to final made-up pages, thus skipping such costly steps as special custom design, multiple stages of proof, and dummying. So far, large commercial publishers have been slow to take advantage of this technology.

Meantime, although the venerable linotype machine has disappeared, many of the old procedures remain in place. The pages that follow address questions that can arise during various stages of a book's production.

— Format —

PLANNING THE TYPE PAGE

It is important for the publisher to take the length of recipes into account when deciding on a cookbook's trim size (the actual dimensions of a book's page). An oblong book, for example, is ideal if most of the recipes are short, but will guarantee bad breaks throughout if they are lengthy.

When planning the cookbook format, the designer should have the entire manuscript in hand so that all the problems can be taken into consideration at once. Alternatively, the editor can select sample pages from the manuscript showing the various elements that will require design decisions. These include the title and contents pages, representative recipes (including longest and shortest), all levels of subheadings, indented text, lists, and so on.

Recipe length is an important factor. The longest recipes should be designed so that—in as many cases as possible—they can fit within a two-page spread, thus avoiding page-turning in mid-recipe. The decision to use a double-column or single-column ingredients list (shown below) will be influenced by this requirement, as will the size of the body type and the use of white space.

Single-column format:	1 cup flour	
	1 cup milk	
	2 eggs	
	Pinch of salt	
	2 tablespoons butter, melted	
Double-column format:	1 cup flour	Pinch of salt
	1 cup milk	2 tablespoons butter,
	2 eggs	melted

AVOIDANCE OF PAGE TURNING

The ideally laid-out cookbook has each recipe complete on a single page or a double-page spread, so that the cook does not have to turn a page in mid-recipe.

The advantages to the cook are obvious. Flipping back and forth from one page to another can be a maddening interruption in a process where concentration is often important. It is particularly difficult if the book is propped up and protected by a plastic cookbook holder.

Editor, production editor, author, and designer should work together at the dummying stage to organize the book so that this ideal can be achieved. The order of recipes may be shifted within a chapter or section. Editor or author may shorten, lengthen, or otherwise adjust the copy to facilitate makeup—always keeping clarity and accuracy in mind. If it is impossible for the designer and editor or author to work face-to-face, the editor should provide the designer with a clear set of guidelines as to which recipes can be moved.

Problems are compounded when recipes are long, detailed, or complicated, or when the book is of small or standard page size. In some books, the ideal is impossible to achieve. But when the publisher is willing to invest some effort, skillful planning and precision can overcome some formidable obstacles. And then no-page-turning can become a selling point for the book, as well as a boon to the consumer.

DUMMYING

All cookbooks—even those without illustrations—should be dummied at the galley-proof stage. (This obviously does not apply to cookbooks whose page makeup has been determined by computer, as discussed on page 165.) In dummying, an uncorrected set of proofs is cut apart recipe by recipe and page by page, to be pasted down on layout boards (sheets of heavy paper that have been ruled off to show the exact size of book and page margins in double-page form). The resulting dummy not only is a guide to the printer, but also shows the position and general appearance of the text as it will be in the finished book.

Some book designers, in order to escape the chore of dummying, resort to ticking off pages (measuring the depth of the column of type and indicating page breaks directly on uncut galley proofs). This practice inevitably leads to mistakes and muddles and in the end can cause delays or costly errors.

Once the dummying is completed and approved and final page numbering has been established, the editor or production editor should insert actual page numbers in the cross-references and contents page, transferring these numbers to the master set of galleys. The index can also be made from a photocopy of the approved dummy rather than from the next stage of proof, allowing the indexer more time to do a careful job.

BAD BREAKS

There are instances when, despite all efforts, a book will have pages that break badly from time to time. But there are some horrors that should be avoided at all costs:

- How-to drawings should never be separated from the related text.
- A list of ingredients should never be placed at the very bottom of a right-hand page or continued from a right-hand page to its reverse. A substantial amount of text relating to the ingredients should be on the same page as the ingredients list.
- A recipe should not break on a right-hand page and continue to the following left-hand page without a continued line (see opposite page) unless it is obvious that the recipe is incomplete as it stands.

ALIGNMENT OF FACING PAGES

In cookbook makeup, it is acceptable practice to align type at the tops of facing pages only, allowing the bottoms to be uneven. Artwork or ornaments can be used to fill particularly large gaps, or spacing between recipes can be varied as necessary.

Perfect alignment at both the top and bottom of facing pages in a cookbook is usually achieved only by running recipes together, one after another, without regard to bad breaks. This is done when space-saving reasons are more important than aesthetics.

CONTINUED LINES

When a recipe must run over from the bottom of a right-hand page to its reverse side, use a continued line to indicate that the recipe is not yet complete. This should appear at the foot of the right-hand page and consist simply of the word *Continued,* set in small type.

Continued lines are particularly important when the recipe appears misleadingly to end—when the main recipe ends at the bottom of a right-hand page, for instance, and is followed on the next page by a note or variation, which might be missed by the reader.

Continued lines are not necessary if the recipe breaks in mid-sentence, since it is then obvious that the recipe continues. They also are not necessary at the foot of a left-hand page when the recipe is continued on the facing page.

TITLE-CONTINUED LINES

When a recipe runs so long that it is separated by one or more pages from its title, it is helpful to run a title-continued line at the upper left of a double-page spread. These small headings can be set in body-type italics or small capitals. The wording consists of the recipe title plus the word *continued.*

> *Fragrant Crispy Duck* (continued)
> FRAGRANT CRISPY DUCK, continued

Title-continued lines are unnecessary when only a fragment of the recipe is carried over to a new left-hand page. But when a substantial portion of the recipe is continued—particularly if it includes the list of ingredients—the line becomes a vital aid to clarity.

Both editor and designer should keep these headings in mind at the dummying stage. It is the responsibility of the editor, copy editor, or production editor to see that they are written on the galley proofs where the dummy indicates they should go.

RUNNING HEADS

Running heads, also known as page heads, are described by the *Chicago Manual of Style* as "signposts telling the reader where he is."

The book, part, or chapter title is repeated at the top of each page, usually on the same line as the page number. If the title is long, a shortened form must be used. A few books have running feet instead; they are exactly the same as running heads except for their position at the foot of the page.

For most large cookbooks, the best choice of headings is the part title on the left-hand page and the chapter title on the right. If the book has long recipes that extend over several pages, the most useful is the chapter title on the left and the recipe title on the right. Running heads in this instance make title-continued lines unnecessary. It is also common to have the chapter title appear on the left-hand page, with no running head on the right-hand page. The least useful choice for a cookbook is to have the running heads consist only of the book title.

— *Typography* —

CHOICE OF TYPEFACE

Many strikingly handsome books can be found in the cooking sections of today's bookstores, a far cry from the practical and often homely designs of the thirties and forties, in which the objective was to cram as much information on a page as possible without regard to aesthetics or convenience to the cook. In contrast, honors are now given for excellence in cookbook design.

The cookbook designer should not lose sight of the fact, however, that the primary purpose of a cookbook is to be read and consulted—and that legibility is of at least the same importance as beauty or dramatic effect. Elaborate design and typographical tricks (such as white type dropping out of a black background) are not recommended for the text portions of a serious cookbook.

Eleven-point type is generally recommended for text and instructions in most cookbooks, with at least two points leading—that is, 11 on 13 or 11/13. This book, for example, is set in 11 on 14 ITC Garamond Book. The list of ingredients can be set ½ point or 1 point smaller if the list is in boldface. If the list is lightface roman or italic, it should be the same size as the text.

ITALIC AND BOLDFACE TYPE

Italics and boldface are commonly used to differentiate a passage from the rest of the text—a visual relief to be picked up by the eye. But italic is not recommended for large blocks of type such as recipe instructions; en masse it is very hard on the eyes.

It can be used with good effect, however, in short pieces of copy. If a cookbook contains only a scattering of headnotes, and if they are only a short paragraph long, italics are permissible.

Italics are used in the text, of course, for some foreign words, for book titles, for names of newspapers and magazines.

Some other items that might be set in italics include the ingredients list, the yield line, small side heads such as notes and variations, and miscellaneous information such as calories and sodium content.

Boldface is used less than italic on a small page, but may be chosen for short headings, yield lines, etc. If it is used for the ingredients list, it may be set smaller than the text (see Choice of Typeface, above).

INGREDIENTS LIST

The designer may decide on a single- or double-column format for the list of ingredients, depending on the size of the book page, the length of the ingredients lines, and the manner in which the recipes are written (some authors prefer a format in which the ingredients and instructions are in adjacent columns).

An important design decision involves the alignment of the elements in the list—a mixture of numbers and words. The clearest form is to have the numbers and fractions "hang," with the ingredient words aligned in a column.

Hanging Numbers

1½ cups milk
½ cup cream
Salt to taste
1 egg
3 cups flour plus additional
for kneading the dough

Perhaps the most elegant look of all is to have as much as an em of space between the hanging numbers column and the word column. This may require special programming by the compositor, however, and the designer should consult with the type house before establishing the design if cost is a factor.

Hanging Numbers with Space

1½ cups milk
½ cup cream
Salt to taste
1 egg
3 cups flour plus additional
for kneading the dough

When double-column ingredients lists are uneven, the longer column should be on the left, to create a sense of balance.

Uneven Columns

1½ cups milk
½ cup cream
Salt to taste
1 egg

3 cups flour plus additional for kneading the dough

But keep units of an ingredient together in a double-column list, even though this can create a lopsided effect.

POOR

1½ cups milk	tional for kneading the
1 egg	dough
3 cups flour plus addi-	

GOOD

1½ cups milk	3 cups flour plus addi-
1 egg	tional for kneading the
	dough

NOTES AND VARIATIONS

Notes, which appear at the end of a recipe and are usually important to the cook, should be set in the same size type as the body of the recipe.

Variations, which are set separately from the main recipe, should also be set in the same size type as the main recipe. When the variation is a complete recipe with its own list of ingredients, the heading should be set smaller than the main recipe title.

When a slight variation creates a separate recipe that should be listed in the index, the editor or author should supply an individual title set in a distinctive manner, even simply italics.

Variations

Blueberry tarts: Substitute 1½ cups rinsed fresh blueberries for the apples and omit the cinnamon.

Peach tarts: Substitute 1½ cups sliced fresh peaches. Omit the cinnamon and add ½ teaspoon almond extract.

When both a note and a variation occur at the end of a recipe, the note precedes the variation.

YIELD LINES

The yield line, or number of servings, is usually set apart from the recipe and printed in different type. It should be styled consistently by the copy editor and keyed for the typesetter. When the yield is included in the text of the recipe, it should appear at the very end of the instructions and may be set in italic.

SPECIAL INFORMATION

Special information—number of calories, sodium content, preparation and cooking times—is often an important feature of cookbooks and figures prominently in the format, even though the designer quite properly chooses a small type size. As with yield lines, this information should be handled consistently by the copy editor and keyed for the typesetter.

Yield: 6 servings

Calories: 324	Fat: 21.9 g
Sodium: 71 mg	Cholesterol: 48 g

Preparation time: 20–25 minutes
Cooking time: 1 hour

SPECIAL SYMBOLS

Typographic devices can save endless repetition of the same phrase throughout the text of recipes. Such phrases include:

May be prepared in advance up to this point.

Available in specialty markets by mail order; see the chapter on Sources for Foreign Ingredients.

Low sodium.

May be frozen at this point.

Suitable for microwave cooking.

The conventional asterisk is the usual symbol for such phrases, but the designer can choose from the dagger (†), the double dagger (‡), the bullet (•), and the star (*), or he can have a special matrix designed for the book.

May be made in an hour or less

This fiery symbol indicates hotness

Conventional symbols available from the compositor's type book are the least expensive. And if the author and editor decide on a special design, the designer may end up pasting hundreds of tiny bits of paper onto reproduction proofs.

The symbols must be explained in the front matter (the pages that precede page 1 of the text). This explanation can be placed alone on a right-hand page, at the end of the contents page, at the end of the author's preface, or at the very end of the front matter. It is worth enclosing in a box so that the reader will not miss it.

Any such symbols are intended more for the frequent user of a book than the browser. The reader who does not know or remember what a symbol means must seek an explanation in the traditional place—the front of the book.

The production editor is responsible for making sure that this explanation for the symbols is properly entered and included with the typescript when it is sent to the compositor. Small items like this, if left until later in the production process, can often be overlooked and can render the recipes confusing at best, or even worthless.

— Illustrations —

Not all cookbooks are illustrated—indeed, not many need to be. In some cookbooks, however, the artwork can be almost as important as the text. This is particularly true of cake and dessert books, for example, where full-color photographs are often used to good advantage; they not only entice the reader into wanting to try a certain recipe but can show far better than words how the finished product should look.

The decision on whether a cookbook is to be illustrated is usually made by the publisher and is based on the editor's and author's projection of what the finished book should look like. Illustrations can be either photographs or drawings; some cookbooks contain both. They may be provided by the author or they may be produced by a professional artist or photographer assigned by the publisher. In the latter case, whether the cost is charged against royalties or is borne by the publisher depends on the contract.

Captions—the titles or descriptions of the illustrations—should accompany all artwork except the merely ornamental. Caption copy is often written in the late stages of production, and the manuscript for it is created in the publishing house (subject to the author's approval). Caption writing can be an art in itself. It is worthwhile for an inexperienced writer to examine a variety of illustrated books and choose the best or most appropriate examples as a model in writing his own.

—9—

Useful Information

— *Table of Equivalents* —

Almonds	1 pound in shell	1¼ cups shelled
	1 pound shelled	3–3½ cups
Anchovy fillets	2-ounce can	10–12 anchovies
Anchovy paste	2-ounce tube	4 tablespoons
Apples	1 pound (3 medium)	2½ cups peeled and sliced
Apricots	1 pound dried	3 cups
	1 pound fresh	8–10 medium
Asparagus	½ pound	6–8 stalks
	1 pound	3½ cups cut into pieces
Bacon	1 pound	30 thin slices
		15 thick slices
		1½ cups diced
Bananas	1 pound (3–4)	1½ cups mashed
		2 cups sliced
Barley	1 cup	3½ cups cooked
Beans, dried	½ pound (1 cup)	2–2½ cups cooked
Beans, fresh shell (fava, cranberry, lima)	1 pound	1 cup shelled
Bean sprouts, fresh	1 pound	3–4 cups
		2 cups cooked
Beets	1 pound, trimmed	2 cups cooked and sliced
	15-ounce can or jar	2 cups sliced
Blueberries	1 pint	2 cups
Bread crumbs	1 slice fresh bread	½ cup coarse crumbs
	1 slice oven-dried	¼ cup fine crumbs
	8-ounce package	2¼ cups
Bulgur	1 cup	3½ cups cooked
Butter	¼ pound (1 stick)	8 tablespoons (½ cup)
	¼ pound	⅓ cup clarified butter

Table of Equivalents (cont.)

Cabbage, regular	2 pounds	9 cups shredded or sliced
		5 cups cooked
Chinese	1½ pounds	6–8 cups sliced
red	2 pounds	4 cups cooked
Carrots, trimmed	1 pound (6–7)	3 cups sliced or shredded
		1⅓ cups cooked and puréed
		2½ cups diced
Cashew nuts	1 pound shelled	3¼ cups
Celery	1 large rib (¼ pound)	½ cup sliced or chopped
Celery root (celeriac)	1 pound	3 cups grated or cut into julienne
		1 cup cooked and puréed
Cheddar cheese	¼ pound	1 cup grated
Cherries	1 pound	2–2½ cups pitted
Chestnuts	1½ pounds in shell	2½ cups peeled
	10-ounce can	about 25 whole chestnuts
Chicken	3½ pounds	3 cups cooked meat
	1 large boned breast	2 cups cooked meat
Chicken broth	13¾-ounce can	1¾ cups
Chick-peas, dried	1 cup	2½ cups cooked
Chocolate	1 ounce (1 square)	2 tablespoons grated
	6-ounce package	1 cup morsels or bits
Clams	3 dozen	4 cups shucked
Cocoa	8-ounce can	2 cups
Coconut	1 medium, fresh	4 cups shredded
		2½ cups coconut milk
	3½-ounce can flaked	1⅓ cups
	4-ounce bag	1⅔ cups
Corn	2 plump ears	1 cup kernels
Cornmeal	1 cup	4 cups cooked
Cornstarch	1 pound	3 cups
Couscous, quick-cooking	1 cup	2½ cups cooked

Crabmeat, fresh	1 pound	3 cups
Cracker and cookie crumbs	28 soda crackers	1 cup
	7 (5 × 2½-inch) graham crackers	1 cup
	22 vanilla wafers	1 cup
	19 chocolate wafers	1 cup
Cranberries	12-ounce bag	3 cups
Cream, heavy	1 cup (½ pint)	2–2½ cups whipped
Cream cheese	3-ounce package	6 tablespoons
Cucumber	2 medium	3 cups sliced
Currants	1 quart fresh	3¾ cups
	10-ounces dried	2 cups
Dates, pitted	8-ounce package	1¼ cups chopped
Eggplant	1½ pounds	2½ cups diced and cooked
Eggs, large	5 whole	1 cup
	1 white	2 tablespoons
	8 whites	1 cup
	1 yolk	1 tablespoon
	12–14 yolks	1 cup
Figs, dried	1 pound	3 cups chopped
Filberts, *see* Hazelnuts		
Flour, all-purpose	¼ ounce	1 tablespoon
	1 pound	3½ cups unsifted
cake	1 pound	4½ cups sifted
whole wheat	1 pound	3½ cups
Garlic	2 medium cloves	1 teaspoon minced
Gelatin	1 envelope (¼ ounce)	1 tablespoon
Ginger, fresh	2-inch piece	2 tablespoons grated or chopped
Grapefruit	1 medium	⅔ cup juice
Grits	1 cup	4 cups cooked
Hazelnuts	1 pound in shell	1½ cups shelled
	1 pound shelled	3½ cups

Table of Equivalents (cont.)

Herbs	1 tablespoon fresh	1 teaspoon dried
Hominy	1 cup	4½ cups cooked
Horseradish	1 tablespoon freshly grated	2 tablespoons bottled
Jerusalem artichokes (sunchokes)	1 pound	2½ cups peeled and sliced
Kasha (buckwheat groats)	1 cup	2½–3 cups cooked
Leeks	2 pounds trimmed	4 cups sliced or chopped
		2 cups cooked
Lemons	1 medium	3 tablespoons juice
		2 teaspoons grated rind
Lentils, dried	1 cup	2½ cups cooked
Limes	1 medium	1½–2 tablespoons juice
		1 teaspoon grated rind
	1 pound (8)	1 cup juice
Lobsters	2 pounds	½ cup cooked meat
Macadamia nuts	7-ounce jar	1½ cups
Macaroni	8 ounces	4 cups cooked
Milk, condensed	14-ounce can	1¼ cups
evaporated	5⅓-ounce can	⅔ cup
Mushrooms	¼ pound fresh	1 cup sliced
		1½ cups chopped
	3 ounces dried	1 pound fresh
Mussels	1 pound	16–20 mussels
Mustard	1 teaspoon dry	1 tablespoon prepared
Nectarines	1 pound (3–4)	2 cups sliced
Noodles	1 pound	7 cups cooked
Nut meats	4 ounces	¾ cup chopped
		1 cup ground

Oats	1 cup	2 cups cooked
Okra	1 pound	22–28 small pods (5 cups)
Onions, yellow	1 medium	½–¾ cup chopped
Oranges	1 medium	⅓ cup juice
		2–3 tablespoons grated rind
Parmesan cheese	¼ pound	1 cup grated
Peaches	1 pound (4 medium)	2 cups peeled and sliced
Peanuts	1 pound in shell	2 cups shelled
	1 pound shelled	3 cups
Pears	1 pound (3 medium)	2 cups sliced
Peas	1 pound in shell	1 cup shelled
	10-ounce package frozen	2 cups
Pecans	1 pound in shell	2 cups shelled
	1 pound shelled	4 cups halved or chopped
Peppers, bell	1 large	1 cup chopped
Pineapple	1 medium	3 cups cubed flesh
Pistachios	1 pound shelled	3½ cups
Plums	1 pound (6 medium)	2½ cups halved and pitted
Potatoes, white	1 pound	3 cups sliced
		1½–2 cups mashed
sweet	1 pound	3 cups sliced
		2 cups mashed
Prunes	1 pound	2½ cups pitted
Pumpkin, fresh	3–4 pounds	3½ cups cooked and puréed
Quince	1 pound (3 medium)	1½ cups chopped
Raisins, seedless	4 ounces	¾ cup
Raspberries	1 pint	1¾–2 cups
Rhubarb	1 pound	2 cups cooked

Table of Equivalents (cont.)

Rice, long-grain white	1 cup	3 cups cooked
brown	1 cup	3–4 cups cooked
wild	1 cup	3 cups cooked
Romano cheese	¼ pound	1 cup grated
Saffron	1/20-ounce vial	1 tablespoon
Scallions	1 bunch (6–7)	⅓ cup chopped (white only)
Scallops	1 pound	2 cups
Shallots	1 large (½ ounce)	1 tablespoon minced
Shortening	1 pound	2½ cups
Shrimp	1 pound	10–15 jumbo
		16–20 large
		25–30 medium
		30–35 small
Sour cream	8 ounces	1 cup
Spinach, fresh	2 pounds loose (or 2 10-ounce bags)	1½ cups cooked and chopped
Split peas	1 cup	2½ cups cooked
Squash, winter	3 pounds	3 cups cooked and puréed
summer	1 pound	3½ cups sliced
		2 cups grated and drained
Strawberries	1 pint	2 cups sliced
Sugar, brown	1 pound	2¼ cups packed
confectioners'	1 pound	3½–4 cups
granulated	1 pound	2¼ cups
Swiss cheese	¼ pound	1 cup shredded
Tomatillos	1 pound (10–12)	2 (13-ounce) cans, drained
Tomatoes	1 pound (3 medium)	1½ cups peeled and seeded
	28-ounce can	2 cups drained pulp
Tomato paste	6-ounce can	¾ cup
	4½-ounce tube	5 tablespoons
Tomato sauce	8 ounces	1 cup
Turnips	1 pound (4)	2½ cups cooked

Walnuts	1 pound in shell	2 cups shelled
	1 pound shelled	3½ cups chopped
Water chestnuts	5-ounce can	15–17 water chestnuts
Wheat germ	12 ounces	3 cups
Yeast	1 (0.6-ounce) cake compressed	1 envelope active dry
	1 envelope active dry	1 scant tablespoon

— Units of Measurement —

Use standard measurement devices to obtain precise amounts.

Measuring spoons for both dry and liquid ingredients come in the following sizes:

¼ teaspoon ½ teaspoon 1 teaspoon 1 tablespoon

Measuring cups for dry ingredients:

¼ cup ⅓ cup ½ cup 1 cup

Measuring cups for liquid ingredients:

8 ounces (1 cup) 16 ounces (2 cups) 1 quart (4 cups)

LARGER VS. SMALLER UNITS OF MEASUREMENT

When there is a choice to be made in specifying a quantity, use the one most easily measured, which is usually the larger unit. An exception is when the ingredient is to be divided (see page 25).

POOR	GOOD
3 teaspoons cinnamon	1 tablespoon cinnamon
4 tablespoons sugar	¼ cup sugar
a 20-cup saucepan	a 5-quart saucepan

— U.S. Measurement Equivalents —

Pinch or dash or few grains	Less than ⅛ teaspoon
1 teaspoon	60 drops; ⅓ tablespoon
3 teaspoons	1 tablespoon
1 tablespoon	½ fluid ounce
2 tablespoons	⅛ cup
3 tablespoons	1 jigger
1 jigger	1½ fluid ounces
4 tablespoons	¼ cup
5⅓ tablespoons	⅓ cup
8 tablespoons	½ cup
½ cup	4 fluid ounces
10⅔ tablespoons	⅔ cup
12 tablespoons	¾ cup
16 tablespoons	1 cup
1 cup	8 fluid ounces
2 cups	1 pint
4 cups	1 quart
8 cups	2 quarts
1 pint	16 fluid ounces
2 pints	1 quart
1 quart	32 fluid ounces
4 quarts	1 gallon
8 quarts	1 peck
4 pecks	1 bushel

— U.S. Can Sizes —

Can sizes were once standardized in the United States; numbered designations were printed on the label to indicate the weight and volume of the contents. A No. 2 can of tomatoes, for example, could be relied upon to contain 2½ cups (20 ounces net weight). Recipes in pre–World War II cookbooks often specified can sizes for quantities in their lists of ingredients.

This practice has been abandoned, partly because manufacturers have taken to changing their can sizes rather than raising their prices, with the result that a bewildering assortment of cans and jars in many sizes can be found on supermarket shelves. Perhaps the most visible evidence of this is the 13-ounce coffee can taking the place of the 16-ounce; one of the least visible is the 11½-ounce can of soup unobtrusively changing to 10¾ ounces.

All of this means, of course, that recipes should state weight and volume of canned foods rather than can sizes. For the convenience of those who are adapting yesterday's recipes for today's readers, the following table lists the most common standard sizes.

Can Size	*Average Weight of Contents*	*Approximate Cupfuls*
No. ¼	4 ounces	½ cup
No. ½	8 ounces	1 cup
No. 1 Tall	10½ ounces	1¼ cups
No. 300	14–16 ounces	1¾–2 cups
No. 303	16–17 ounces	2 cups
No. 2	20 ounces	2½ cups
No. 2½	29 ounces	3½ cups
No. 3	46 ounces	5¾ cups
No. 10	106 ounces	13 cups

—*Measurements for Drinks*—

Measurement	*Equivalent*
1 dash	6 drops
2 tablespoons	1 ounce
1 pony	1 ounce
1 finger	1 ounce
1 jigger	1½–2 ounces

— Liquor Bottle Capacities —

The liquor industry has completely converted to the metric system.

Former Size	U.S. Fluid Ounces	New Size	U.S. Fluid Ounces
1 pint	16	500 ml	16.9
1 fifth (4/5 quart)	25.6	750 ml	25.4
1 quart	32	1 l	33.8
½ gallon	64	1¾ l	59.2

— Wine Bottle Capacities —

Size	U.S. Ounces	Liters
Split	6.3	187 ml
Half bottle	12.7	375 ml
Standard bottle*	25.4	750 ml
Liter	33.8	1
Magnum	50.7	1½

Jeroboam	equals 4 standard bottles
Rehoboam	equals 6 standard bottles
Methuselah	equals 8 standard bottles
Salmanazar	equals 12 standard bottles
Balthazar	equals 16 standard bottles
Nebuchadnezzar	equals 20 standard bottles

*Slightly less than former U.S. fifth.

— *Standard Pan Sizes* —

	Pan Size	Approximate Volume
Cake pans		
round	8 × 1½ inches	4 cups
	9 × 2 inches	6 cups
rectangular	13 × 9 × 2 inches	15 cups
square	8 × 2 inches	8 cups
	9 × 1½ inches	8 cups
	9 × 2 inches	10 cups
tube	9 × 3 inches	12 cups
	10 × 4 inches	18 cups
Loaf pans	8½ × 4½ × 2½ inches	6 cups
	9 × 5 × 3 inches	8 cups
Pie pans	8 × 1¼ inches	3 cups level
	9 × 1½ inches	4 cups level
	9 × 2 inches (deep dish)	6 cups level
Tart or quiche pans	4 × 1¼ inches	½ cup
	8 × 1 inch	1½ cups
	9 × 1⅜ inches	4 cups
Soufflé dishes	varying sizes	1½ to 8 cups
Savarin mold	9½ inch round	6 cups
Springform pan	8 × 3 inches	12 cups
	9 × 3 inches	16 cups
Charlotte molds	7 × 4 inches	8 cups
Ramekins	3 × 1½ inches	½ cup

—*Measuring Dry Ingredients*— *by Weight*

The European system of measuring by weight rather than by volume is gaining more proponents in the United States, but mostly among food writers. Because weight is more precise than cups, it is especially helpful in baking.

The author who chooses this system must, however, make sure the quantities are accurately expressed in cups as well as weight to make the recipes useful. (American readers generally do not use kitchen scales and no amount of proselytizing will change them.) This should be done during the testing of recipes, rather than merely translating the ounces into cups at a later date. The conversion is laborious for the editor to do and will not be as accurate.

When dual measurements are used, they should be given for both liquids and solids. The exception is quantities that can be measured in tablespoonfuls and teaspoonfuls, which cannot be weighed accurately and need no translation.

Choose a style that is as unobtrusive as possible.

Cups/Ounces	*Ounces/Cups*
6 large eggs	6 large eggs
¾ cup (5½ ounces) sugar	5½ ounces (¾ cup) sugar
1 cup (5 ounces) flour	5 ounces (1 cup) flour
½ teaspoon vanilla extract	½ teaspoon vanilla extract
4 tablespoons butter	4 tablespoons butter
½ cup (4 ounces) olive oil	4 ounces (½ cup) olive oil

— *U.S. vs. Foreign Measures* —

There are a few notable differences between American and foreign systems of measurement that concern food writers and editors:

Dry ingredients are measured by weight in most countries rather than by the cupfuls used in the United States.

The rest of the world is firmly on the metric system while Americans cling to the linear.

British liquid measure is based on the Imperial gallon; therefore the British standard pints and quarts are different from those in the United States.

— *Metrics* —

The international metric system is based on three principal units: the meter for measuring length, the gram for weight, and the liter for capacity.

A spirited campaign to educate the American public in the use of metrics began in this country when the Metric Conversion Act became federal law in 1975. Metrics were taught in the schools, attempts were made to change highway signs from miles to kilometers, and publishers began using the metric system in texts side by side with American Standard (linear). It was hoped that the nation could be converted to the metric system by 1985.

The campaign met with such relentless resistance, however, that it has ground to a virtual halt. But it has left some debris. A dual system of measurement is in use for grocery labeling, liquors come in liters rather than quarts, and metric conversion tables are often found in the back pages of cookbooks.

This may change with the emergence of the European Community, when publishers hope to find markets on both sides of the Atlantic, but for now it is the rare author who chooses to express measurements in both metric and American Standard.

— General Formula for— Metric Conversion

Ounces to grams	multiply ounces by 28.35
Grams to ounces	multiply grams by .035
Pounds to grams	multiply pounds by 453.5
Pounds to kilograms	multiply pounds by .45
Cups to liters	multiply cups by .24
Fahrenheit to centigrade	subtract 32 from Fahrenheit, multiply by 5, then divide by 9
Centigrade to Fahrenheit	multiply centigrade by 9, divide by 5, then add 32

General Table of Metric Equivalents (Volume and Weight)

Volume	
1 ounce	28.35 grams
1 pound	453.59 grams
1 gram	.035 ounces
1 kilogram	2.2 pounds
Weight	
1 cup	16 tablespoons
	8 fluid ounces
	236.6 milliliters
1 tablespoon	3 teaspoons
	.5 fluid ounce
	14.8 milliliters
1 teaspoon	4.9 milliliters
1 liter	1000.0 milliliters
	1.06 quarts
1 bushel	4 pecks
1 peck	8 quarts

Weight *(cont.)*

1 gallon	4 quarts
1 quart	2 pints
1 pint	2 cups
	473.2 milliliters

—*Approximate Metric Equivalents by Weight*—

U.S.	*Metric*
¼ ounce	7 grams
½ ounce	14 grams
1 ounce	28 grams
1¼ ounces	35 grams
1½ ounces	40 grams
1⅔ ounces	45 grams
2 ounces	55 grams
2½ ounces	70 grams
4 ounces	112 grams
5 ounces	140 grams
8 ounces	228 grams
10 ounces	280 grams
15 ounces	425 grams
16 ounces (1 pound)	454 grams

Metric	*U.S.*
1 gram	.035 ounce
50 grams	1.75 ounces
100 grams	3.5 ounces
250 grams	8.75 ounces
500 grams	1.1 pounds
1 kilogram	2.2 pounds

—Approximate Metric Equivalents— by Volume

U.S.	Metric
¼ cup	60 milliliters (0.56 deciliters)
⅓ cup	80 milliliters (0.75 deciliters)
½ cup	120 milliliters (1.13 deciliters)
⅔ cup	160 milliliters (1.5 deciliters)
1 cup	230 milliliters (2.27 deciliters)
1¼ cups	300 milliliters
1½ cups	360 milliliters
1⅔ cups	400 milliliters
2 cups	460 milliliters
2½ cups	600 milliliters
3 cups	700 milliliters (6.81 deciliters)
4 cups (1 quart)	.95 liter
1.06 quarts	1 liter
4 quarts (1 gallon)	3.8 liters

Metric	U.S.
50 milliliters	.21 cup
100 milliliters	.42 cup
150 milliliters	.63 cup
200 milliliters	.84 cup
250 milliliters	1.06 cups
1 liter	1.05 quarts

— *Approximate Metric Equivalents by Length* —

U.S.	Metric
1/8 inch	.3 centimeters
1/4 inch	.6 centimeters
1 inch	2.5 centimeters
2 inches	5.08 centimeters
4 inches	10.16 centimeters
5 inches	13 centimeters
6 inches	15.24 centimeters
8 inches	20.32 centimeters
9 inches	22.86 centimeters
10 inches	25.4 centimeters
12 inches	30.48 centimeters
14 inches	35.56 centimeters
16 inches	40.64 centimeters
20 inches	50.8 centimeters

— *British and U.S. Fluid Volume Equivalents* —

The Imperial gallon, adopted by the British in the mid-nineteenth century, is based on a gallon of water that weighs 10 pounds rather than on the approximately 8⅓ pounds it weighs in the United States.

Imperial	U.S.
1 ounce	.96 ounce
1 pint	19.2 ounces
1 quart	38.4 ounces

— British and U.S. Cooking Terms —

British	U.S. Equivalent
aubergine	eggplant
beetroot	beet
bilberry	blueberry
biscuit	cracker or cookie
broad bean	fava bean
chips	french-fried potatoes
cling film	plastic wrap
collops	meatballs
cornflour	cornstarch
courgette	zucchini
cream, double	heavy cream
cream, single	light cream
crisps	potato chips
dripping	fat from roasted meat
fish slice	spatula
flour, maize	cornmeal
flour, strong	bread flour; hard-wheat flour
forcemeat	stuffing mixture for meat or fish
french bean	green bean
gammon	ham
golden syrup	substitute light corn syrup
groundnut	peanut
hand of pork	pork shoulder roast
heaped spoonful	heaping spoonful
joint	large cut of meat with bone; roast
mince (n.)	ground meat
offal	variety meats (liver, heart, kidney)
pasty (n.)	savory turnover
pie dish	deep baking dish
pig's trotter	pig's foot
pine kernels	pine nuts
pips	seeds
pluck (n.)	heart, liver, and lights (lungs)

British	*U.S. Equivalent*
pudding	dessert
sack	sweet sherry
stoned	seeded
sugar, caster	superfine granulated
sugar, icing	confectioners' sugar
sultanas	golden raisins
treacle	molasses
tunny	tuna
vegetable marrow	squash

— *Translating Foreign Measures* — *(Approximate Equivalents)*

Substance	*Grams*	*Ounces*	*Cups*
Butter	30	1	⅛ (2 tablespoons)
	55	2 (½ stick)	¼ (4 tablespoons)
	70	2½	⅓ (5⅓ tablespoons)
	100	3¾	½ less 1 tablespoon
	110	4 (1 stick)	½ (8 tablespoons)
	140	5	⅔ (10⅔ tablespoons)
	150	5¾	½ plus 3 tablespoons
	220	8 (2 sticks)	1 (16 tablespoons)
	275	10 (2½ sticks)	1¼ (20 tablespoons)
	330	12 (3 sticks)	1½ (24 tablespoons)
	454	16 (4 sticks)	2 (32 tablespoons)
Flour	35	1¼	¼
(all-purpose)	45	1⅔	⅓
	70	2½	½
	90	3⅓	⅔
	110	4	¾

Substance	*Grams*	*Ounces*	*Cups*
Flour *(cont.)*	140	5	1
(all-purpose)	175	6¼	1¼
	210	7½	1½
	280	10	2
	350	12½	2½
	520	15	3
	560	20 (1¼ pounds)	4
Sugar	50	2	¼
(granulated)	65	2½	⅓
	100	3½	½
	130	5	⅔
	200	7	1
	250	9	1¼
	300	11	1½
	330	12	1⅔
	400	14	2
	450	16 (1 pound)	2½

—*Egg Grades and Sizes*—

Grades

U.S. Grade AA (Fancy Fresh Quality)
U.S. Grade A

Sizes

Jumbo	30 ounces and up per dozen
Extra-large	27–30 ounces per dozen
Large	24–27 ounces per dozen
Medium	21–24 ounces per dozen
Small	18–21 ounces per dozen

— Butter by Weight and Measure* —

Pounds	Ounces	Tablespoons	Sticks	Cups
1/16	1	2	¼	⅛
—	1½	3	—	—
⅛	2	4	½	¼
—	2½	5	—	—
⅙	2⅔	5⅓	—	⅓
—	3	6	—	—
—	3½	7	—	—
¼	4	8	1	½
—	4½	9	—	—
—	5	10	—	⅝
⅓	5⅓	10⅔	—	⅔
—	5½	11	—	—
—	6	12	1½	¾
—	6½	13	—	—
—	7	14	—	⅞
—	7½	15	—	—
½	8	16	2	1
—	8½	17	—	—
—	9	18	—	1⅛
—	9½	19	—	—
⅝	10	20	2½	1¼
—	10½	21	—	—
⅔	10⅔	21⅓	—	1⅓
—	11	22	—	—
¾	12	24	3	1½
—	13	26	—	1⅝
⅞	14	28	3½	1¾
—	15	30	—	1⅞
1	16	32	4	2

***As discussed on page 17, butter measurements are best given in tablespoons or ounces and sticks. Measuring by the cup is not recommended. This table gives cup measurements as an aid in conversion.**

— Types of Milk and Cream —

FRESH FLUID MILKS

Raw milk: unpasteurized; sold in health food stores
Homogenized milk: butterfat particles have been broken up and distributed evenly throughout
Whole milk: contains about 3.5 percent butterfat
Skim milk: contains less than 0.5 percent butterfat
Low-fat milk, 2 percent: has 98 percent of the butterfat removed
Low-fat milk, 1 percent: has 99 percent of the butterfat removed
Buttermilk: low-fat or nonfat milk with tangy flavor and slightly thickened texture
Ultrapasteurized milk: heated to 300 degrees F, then vacuum-packed; needs refrigeration only after opening

CANNED MILKS

Evaporated milk: unsweetened homogenized milk from which about 60 percent of the water has been removed
Evaporated skim milk: contains 0.5 percent butterfat
Sweetened condensed milk: a sticky, sweet blend of evaporated whole milk and sugar

POWDERED MILK

Powdered whole milk: dried whole milk; must be refrigerated
Nonfat dry milk: dried milk from which almost all butterfat has been removed
Powdered buttermilk: desiccated buttermilk; used in baking

CREAMS

Light whipping cream: most commonly available; contains 30 to 36 percent butterfat

Heavy whipping cream: contains 36 to 40 percent butterfat

Light cream or coffee cream: contains about 20 percent butterfat; will not whip

Half-and-half: half milk and half light cream; contains 10 to 12 percent butterfat; will not whip

Sour cream: light cream that has been commercially soured; contains about 20 percent butterfat

Ultrapasteurized cream: heated to 300 degrees F to retard spoilage; has a long shelf life but does not whip as well and taste has been slightly affected

— *Types of Flour* —

(Note that most flours on the market today have been presifted.)

COMMONLY USED FLOURS (AVAILABLE IN MOST SUPERMARKETS)

All-purpose bleached

All-purpose unbleached

Bread flour: hard-wheat flour, high in gluten

Cake flour: soft-wheat flour, low in gluten; sometimes available as self-rising flour

Graham flour: coarse whole wheat flour

Instant flour: granular flour used for thickening; treated so it does not lump

Pastry flour: soft-wheat flour, low in gluten

Rye flour: heavy, dark, low in gluten; sometimes sold as "medium rye flour"

Self-rising flour: white flour with salt and baking powder added; to be used only in recipes specifically calling for it

Whole wheat flour: finely milled wheat flour with wheat germ intact

SPECIAL FLOURS (AVAILABLE IN HEALTH FOOD STORES OR SPECIALTY MARKETS)

Barley
Brown rice
Buckwheat
Corn (masa harina)
Gluten
Lentil
Oat
Pumpernickel (rye meal)
Rice
Semolina
Soy
Triticale
Water chestnut

— *Sugars and Other Sweeteners* —

SUGARS

Brown sugar: granulated white sugar that has been moistened with molasses; available in light or more strongly flavored dark; must be firmly packed when measured

Confectioners' or powdered sugar: very finely pulverized granulated sugar mixed with a small amount of cornstarch

Granulated or white sugar: refined all-purpose sugar made from cane or sugar beets; 99 percent pure

Maple sugar: concentrated maple syrup that has crystallized

Raw sugar: a coarse-grained by-product of molasses, available as the moist Barbados and the dry Demerara

Superfine sugar: extra-fine grain granulated sugar; fast dissolving

SYRUPS

Corn syrup: a thick sweet syrup made from hydrolized cornstarch; available in light and dark

Golden syrup: evaporated sugarcane juice; popular in the South and in England

Honey: flower nectar converted to syrupy consistency by bees

Maple syrup: concentrated sap of the sugar maple tree

Molasses: dark and distinctly flavored syrup made from sugarcane or sugar beet juice

Sorghum molasses: a syrup made from the sap of the cereal grass sorghum

LOW-CALORIE SWEETENERS

Aspartame: a synthetic sweetener made from amino acids; not to be used in baking but is an excellent sweetener for cold desserts

Saccharin: a sugar substitute in use for almost a century; may be used in cooking if other adjustments are made for loss in bulk; now controversial and still being researched by USDA

— *Types of Salt* —

Coarse salt: a term applied to any coarse-grained salt, such as kosher, rock, and sea salt

Kosher salt: the purest salt available; contains no additives and is at least 99.9 percent pure to qualify for certification as kosher; not recommended for cake baking because of coarse crystals

Pickling salt: a fine-grained pure salt containing no additives and used in making pickles because it will not turn cloudy

Rock salt: unrefined salt that comes in grayish, chunky crystals; used mostly for nonflavoring purposes, such as a salt bed for oysters or clams

Sea salt: evaporated sea water containing minerals and natural impurities, with bigger and harder crystals than kosher salt; when used at the table it should be ground in a salt mill

Table salt: our most commonly used salt, fine in texture and very salty in taste; often mixed with additives such as magnesium or sodium carbonate to make it flow more easily; more than twice as intense in flavor as coarse salt

— Types of Rice —

Arborio: generic name of the most often imported variety of Italian rice, which has a short, thick grain; preferred for risottos

Basmati: a fragrant long-grained rice that grows best in India; should be washed and soaked before cooking

Brown rice: unpolished rice with only the husk removed and thus more nutritious than white rice; treated like white rice but with a longer cooking time

Converted rice: rice that has been steam-treated; cook according to package directions

Glutinous rice: an Asian short-grained rice that becomes very sticky when cooked

Mochi: a high-starch short-grained Japanese rice that is extremely sticky when cooked; used in some desserts and in making rice flour

White rice: polished long-grain or short-grain rice with the germ, bran, and husk removed; our most commonly used rice

— Chicken Sizes and Weights —

Classification	*Weight*
Squab chicken (poussin)	Approximately 1 pound
Broiler-fryer	2 to 3½ pounds (for all-purpose use)
Roaster	4 to 8 pounds
Capon	4 to 10 pounds
Fowl (stewing hen)	3 to 6 pounds

—Poultry and Game Birds:— Amounts per Average Serving

Kind of Bird	*Amount to Allow per Person*
Chicken	
whole	12 ounces
parts	8 to 10 ounces
Turkey	
under 12 pounds	¾ pound
12 pounds or over	½ pound to ¾ pound
parts	½ pound
Duck	
under 4 pounds	1 duck serves 2
4 pounds or over	1 duck serves 2 to 3
Goose	
whole	1 to 1½ pounds
Game Hen	
whole	½ to 1 bird per person
Squab	
whole	1 squab per person
Pheasant	
whole (2 to 3 pounds)	1 pheasant serves 2
Quail	
whole (5 ounces each)	2 quail per person
Partridge	
whole (12 to 14 ounces)	1 partridge per person

— *U.S. Beef Cuts* —

Names Commonly Used	*Other Names Used Regionally*
arm pot roast	cross rib roast/thick rib roast/thick end roast/round bone roast/shoulder roast/round shoulder roast
blade pot roast	chuck roast/blade cut chuck roast/square cut chuck roast/English cut roast/7 roast/7-bone roast/flat bone roast
boneless sirloin steak	top loin steak/hip steak/rump steak/top of Iowa steak/top sirloin butt steak/bottom sirloin butt steak
bottom/outside round	silverside/gooseneck/silver tip/Swiss steak
brisket	deckle/boneless brisket/bone-in brisket/fresh boneless brisket/beef breast/brisket pot roast/barbeque beef brisket/corned beef
chuck/short ribs	flanken/brust flanken
chuck tender	scotch tender/Jewish tender/kosher filet/round muscle/fish muscle/top eye pot roast/catfish pot roast
club steak	sirloin steak/sirloin strip steak/Delmonico steak/market steak/individual steak
English cut	Boston cut/bread and butter/boneless English cut
flank steak	London broil/cube steak/minute steak/flank steak filet/Swiss steak

Names Commonly Used	*Other Names Used Regionally*
fore shank	shin/fore shin/shank
heel of round	pike's peak/diamond wedge/gooseneck/ horseshoe/upper round/ lower round/Jew daube/ Denver pot roast
loin strip steak	top loin steak/sirloin steak/boneless sirloin steak/New York steak/Kansas City steak/club steak/Delmonico steak/shell steak/strip steak/boneless top sirloin steak/boneless hotel steak/boneless hip steak/minute sirloin steak/key strip steak
mechanically tenderized steaks	cubed steak/chicken steak/minute steak/quick steak/sandwich steak
porterhouse steak	T-bone steak/large T-bone steak/tenderloin steak/king steak
rib eye steak	market steak/spencer steak/beauty steak/Delmonico steak/boneless Delmonico steak/center cut steak/boneless rib steak/club steak/boneless club steak/boneless rib club steak/country club steak/regular roll steak
round	bucket steak/top round/bottom round/eye of round/full cut round/Swiss steak
short ribs	middle ribs/English short ribs

Names Commonly Used	*Other Names Used Regionally*
shoulder clod	scalped shoulder/shoulder roast/boneless shoulder/cross rib/rolled cross rib/clod roast/boneless clod roast/London broil
sirloin, loin end	hip/short hip/head loin/rump/K-style butt/sirloin butt bone-in/sirloin butt/sir butt/sirloin butt/family steak
sirloin tip/knuckle	short sirloin/top sirloin/sirloin butt/crescent/veiny/bell of knuckle/face/face rump/round/boneless sirloin/round tip/ball tip/loin tip/family steak/sandwich steak
skirt steak	skirt steak filet
T-bone steak	porterhouse steak/small T-bone steak/club steak/tenderloin steak
tenderloin	filet mignon/petite filet/tenderloin roast/tenderloin tips/tips

—Meat: Amounts per Average Serving—

Cut of Meat	Amount to Allow per Person
Beef	
rib roast, bone in	12 ounces
rib roast, boneless	6 to 8 ounces
pot roast, bone in	8 to 12 ounces
pot roast, boneless	6 to 8 ounces
stewing beef, bone in	8 to 12 ounces
stewing beef, boneless	6 to 8 ounces
stewing beef, bony (short ribs, etc.)	12 to 16 ounces
steaks, bone in	8 to 12 ounces
steaks, boneless	6 to 8 ounces
ground beef	6 to 8 ounces
Lamb	
roast leg or shoulder, bone in	12 to 16 ounces
roast leg or shoulder, boneless	6 to 8 ounces
rack or rib roast	1 rack serves 2 persons
crown roast	2 ribs per serving
chops, shoulder	1 chop per person
chops, loin	1 or 2 chops per person
chops, rib	2 or 3 chops per person
shanks	1 per person
ground lamb	6 ounces
Pork	
roast, bone in	12 to 16 ounces
roast, boneless	6 to 8 ounces
chops	1 or 2 chops per person
spareribs	12 to 16 ounces
suckling pig	1¼ pounds
pig's feet and hocks	1 pound

Cut of Meat	*Amount to Allow per Person*
Veal	
roast loin or rib, bone in	12 to 16 ounces
boneless roast	6 to 8 ounces
chops	1 loin or rib chop, 1 inch thick
scaloppine	4 to 6 ounces
shanks	12 to 16 ounces
Variety Meats	
heart	8 ounces
kidneys	6 to 8 ounces
liver	4 to 6 ounces
oxtail	12 to 16 ounces
sweetbreads and brains	4 to 6 ounces
tongue	4 to 6 ounces
tripe	4 to 6 ounces

— *Meat Roasting Chart** —

Meat	*Internal Temperature When Removed from Oven*
Beef	
rare	120°–125°F
medium rare	130–140
medium	145–150
well done	155–165
Veal	
well done	155–160
Lamb	
rare	130–135
medium rare	140–145

*Meat will continue cooking after it is removed from the oven, and the internal temperature will continue to increase by approximately 5 degrees. The temperatures indicated above are based on this fact; all roast meats should rest at least 15 minutes before being carved—up to 30 minutes for large roasts.

medium	150–160
well done	160–165
Pork	
fresh	140–150
cured (uncooked)	140–150
cured (ready to eat)	130
Poultry	
chicken	180–185
turkey	180–185

— Fresh Fish and Shellfish: — Amounts per Average Serving

Kind of Fish	*Amount to Allow per Person*
Fish	
Whole, gutted	¾ to 1 pound
Whole, dressed	8 ounces
Fillets, steaks	6 to 8 ounces
Frogs' Legs	
Pairs (2 to 8 ounces)	3 to 6 legs
Shellfish	
Clams: steamers	20 clams
hard shell	2 dozen serves 4 to 6 as appetizers
large chowder	1 quart shucked makes 6 portions
in shell	8 quarts makes 1 quart shucked
Crabmeat, cooked	1 pound (3 cups) serves 3 to 4
Crabs, soft shell	2 to 3 crabs
Mussels: in shell	3 quarts makes 4 servings
shucked	1 quart (undrained) makes 4 servings
Oysters: on half shell	6 to 12 per person, depending on size
shucked	1 to 1½ quarts (36 to 48) serves 6
Shrimp, in shell	6 to 8 ounces
Squid	8 ounces

— Oven Temperatures: — British and U.S.

Heat Level	Degrees Fahrenheit	Degrees Centigrade	British (Regulo) Gas Mark
Very cool	200	95	0
Very cool	225	110	¼
Very cool	250	120	½
Cool or slow	275	135	1
Cool or slow	300	150	2
Warm	325	165	3
Moderate	350	175	4
Moderately hot	375	190	5
Fairly hot	400	200	6
Hot	425	220	7
Very hot	450	230	8
Very hot	475	245	9

— Herbs, Spices, and Aromatics —

The difference between an herb and a spice originally was whether it was grown in the tropics (in which case it was a spice) or in a temperate climate (an herb). Today the word spice is more conveniently used to include all dried aromatic seeds as well as the original spices shipped from the Orient, and it can also cover dried chilies from America. Aromatics are vegetables that are used to give flavors to other foods they are cooked with.

Dried herbs are more pungent than fresh. In making substitutions, figure on one third to one half the amount of a dried herb substituted for a fresh one.

HERBS

Basil
Bay leaf
Borage
Chervil
Chive*
Cilantro (fresh coriander)
Dill weed
Marjoram
Mint
Oregano
Parsley
Rosemary
Sage
Savory
Tarragon
Thyme

SPICES

Allspice
Anise
Caraway
Cardamom
Cayenne (red pepper)
Celery seed
Chili powder
Cinnamon
Clove
Coriander
Cumin
Curry powder
Dill seed
Fennel
Ginger
Juniper
Mace
Mustard
Nutmeg
Paprika
Pepper
Poppy seed
Saffron
Sesame seed
Turmeric

AROMATICS

Carrot
Celery
Garlic
Horseradish
Onion
Shallot
Vanilla bean

*Strictly speaking, chive is not an herb but a member of the lily family.

— Substitutions —

Ingredient	*Substitute*
Butter	
2 sticks (1/2 pound)	2/3 cup rendered chicken fat
2 sticks (1/2 pound)	7/8 cup vegetable oil
2 sticks (1/2 pound)	7/8 cup lard
Eggs	
1 whole egg	2 egg yolks plus 1 tablespoon water (for use in baking)
2 egg yolks	1 whole egg (for custards, mayonnaise, other sauces)
Flour	
1 cup all-purpose flour	1 cup plus 2 tablespoons cake flour
1 cup cake flour	7/8 cup (1 cup less 2 tablespoons) all-purpose flour
1 cup self-rising flour	1 cup all-purpose flour plus 1 1/4 teaspoons baking powder and a pinch of salt
Leavening	
1 teaspoon double-acting baking powder	1/4 teaspoon baking soda plus 1/2 teaspoon cream of tartar
1 envelope (1/4 ounce) dry yeast	1 scant tablespoon dry yeast
1 small cake (0.6 ounce) fresh yeast	1 envelope dry yeast
1 large cake (2 ounces) fresh yeast	3 small (0.6 ounce) cakes fresh or 3 envelopes (1/4 ounce each) dry yeast
Milk and Cream	
1 cup whole milk	1 cup skim milk plus 2 teaspoons melted butter
1 cup fresh milk	1/2 cup evaporated milk plus 1/2 cup water

Ingredient	*Substitute*
1 cup fresh milk	⅓ cup nonfat dry milk plus ¾ cup water plus 2 teaspoons melted butter
1 cup fresh milk	1 cup sour milk or buttermilk plus ½ teaspoon baking soda
1 cup skim milk	⅓ cup nonfat dry milk plus ¾ cup water
1 cup light cream	¾ cup milk plus 3 tablespoons melted butter
1 cup sour cream	1 cup plain yogurt
1 cup sour cream	1 cup evaporated milk plus 1 tablespoon lemon juice
Sweeteners	
1 cup granulated sugar	⅞ cup honey
1 cup granulated sugar	1 cup maple syrup plus ¼ cup corn syrup
1 cup light corn syrup or honey	1¼ cups granulated sugar plus ⅓ cup liquid
1 cup granulated sugar	1 cup molasses plus 1 teaspoon baking soda
Thickening Agents	
1 tablespoon arrowroot	2½ tablespoons all-purpose flour
1 tablespoon cornstarch	2 tablespoons all-purpose flour
1 tablespoon potato flour	2 tablespoons all-purpose flour
1 tablespoon tapioca	1½ tablespoons all-purpose flour

—10—

Word List

New words come into the language and spellings change faster than dictionaries can issue revised editions. There are also words that are not included in dictionaries because they are in limited usage. The following list of food words can serve as a spelling reference for writers and editors, but the dictionary should be close at hand.

The French Academy has proposed a simplification of spelling of many French words so that students can devote less time to idiosyncratic spellings and more time to other academic subjects. *Oignon* would become *ognon,* hyphens would be dropped in many words, and the circumflex would also be limited to only a few words. The dispute that developed after the proposal, however, means that it will be many years before the changes are enacted, if ever.

Foreign words with asterisks indicate that they are not in Webster's Third New International Dictionary or Webster's Ninth New Collegiate Dictionary, the two standard references for publishers of books, magazines, and newspapers, or in the second edition of the unabridged Random House Dictionary. (We have included Random House because it lists many culinary terms not in Webster's.) The foreign words can be italicized or not, according to the preferred style for each manuscript.

We disagree with some of the recommended spellings, and the writer and editor can as well. The lexicographers even disagree among themselves. Webster's prefers catsup, Random House prefers ketchup. Webster's also does not use an accent for puree, although it does for sauté. Random House uses both accents. We do not have the equivalent of the French Academy to protect the English language, but our major dictionaries are the nearest equivalent. They are not sacrosanct, however, and one can choose to differ. This is especially true with transliterations.

A.1. steak sauce
*abbachio
achiote
*acini di pepe
ackee, *see* akee
adobo
adzuki
*aemono
agar (*also* agar-agar)
*agedashi
*agemono
*aglio e olio
agnolotti
*agro dolce
aguardiente
*aigre-doux
aioli
*ajo
akee
akvavit, *see* aquavit
à la carte
à la king
à la mode
*albóndigas
Albufera
al dente
alfresco
*alioli
*all'Amatriciana
*allumettes
amandine
amaretti *(the cookies)*
amaretto *(the liqueur)*
*américaine
*amorini
*amuse-gueule
anadama bread
ancho chili
andouille, andouillette
angel food cake
angel hair pasta
angels on horseback
angostura bitters
*anguilles
aniseed
annatto
antipasto
*antojitos
apéritif
*apfelstrudel
appenzeller
applejack
apple pandowdy
applesauce
aquavit
*arancini
arborio rice
*argenteuil
Armagnac
*arrabbiata

*Asterisks indicate words that do not appear in Webster's or in the Random House Dictionary.

arroz con pollo
arugula
asafetida
aubergine
au gratin
au jus
avgolemono
avocado(s)

baba(s)
baba au rhum
baba ghanouj
babka
bacalao *(Spanish)*, baccalà *(Italian)*
backbone
bagel
Baggie
*bagna caôda (*also* bagna cauda)
baguette
bain-marie
baked Alaska
Bake-Off
baklava
*ballekes
ballottine
*balsamella
balsamic vinegar
barbecue
bar-le-duc
barquettes
Bartlett pear
basmati rice
*basquaise
*basturma
battuto
Bavarian cream
*bavettine
béarnaise sauce
Beau Monde seasoning
béchamel
beefsteak
beef stroganoff
beef Wellington
beggar's chicken, beggar's purses
beignet
Belgian endive
*belle-Hélène
bell pepper
Bel Paese
beluga caviar
benne wafers
*berner platte
beurre blanc
beurre manié
beurre noir
beurre noisette
*bhuna gosht
bialy(s)
Bibb lettuce
*biersuppe
bigarade
Big Mac
*bigos
billi-bi
Bing cherry
bird's-nest soup
*biryani
biscotto *(sing.)*, biscotti *(pl.)*
biscuit

bisque
*bistecca
black bottom pie
black-eyed pea
Black Forest cake
blancmange
blanquette
blin *(sing.)*, blini *(pl.)*
blintze
Bloody Mary
*bocconcini
*bockwurst
bok choy
boletus
*bollito misto
bologna
bolognese
Bombay duck
bombe
bonbon
bonito
bonne femme
bordelaise
borscht
Bosc pear
Boston baked beans
Boston lettuce
boudin
bouillabaisse
bouillon
*boulangère
*bouquetière
bouquet garni
bourbon
bourguignonne (bourguignon *often used when combined with English*)
bourride
Boursault
*boursin
braciola
*brandade de morue
brandy
bratwurst
braunschweiger
Brazil nut
bread-and-butter pickle
bread crumbs
breadfruit
breadstick
breastbone
*bresaola
brewer's yeast
Brie
*brik
brisling
broccoli rape *or* rabe
brochette
*brodo
Brunswick stew
*bruschetta
brussels sprouts
brynza
*b'steeya (*also* pastilla)
bubble and squeak
*bubliki
*bucati, bucatini
*bûche de noël
Buffalo chicken wings
bulgur
*bündnerfleisch
Bundt pan
buñuelo(s)
*buraki
*burekakia
burgoo

*burrida
burrito(s)
butter bean
butter clam
buttercream
butterfat
butterfish
buttermilk
butternut squash
butterscotch

cabrito
cacciatore
*cacciucco
Caesar salad
café *(French and Spanish),*
caffè *(Italian)*
café au lait
café brûlot
café con leche
café filtre
café noir
caffeine
Cajun
calamari
calamata, *see* kalamata
*caldo verde
calf's feet, liver, tongue
callaloo
Calvados
calzone *(sing. and pl.)*
camomile, *see* chamomile
canapé
*caneton
canister
*cannellini
cannelloni
cannoli
canola oil
cantaloupe
Cape gooseberry
capelli d'angelo
*capellini
capilotade
caponata
cappelletti
cappuccino
carambola
caramelize
carbonara
carbonnade
*carciofi
cardamom
cardoon
Carême
*carne asada
*carpaccio
*carré d'agneau
*carrozza
cartilage
casaba melon
*casalinga
cascabel
*cassata
cassava
cassia
cassis; crème de cassis
cassoulet
*castagnacciocatfish
catsup, *see* ketchup
caul fat

*cavatelli
cayenne
cebiche, *see* seviche
ceci
celeriac
*céleri rémoulade
cèpe
cervelat
*cervelle
ceviche, *see* seviche
Chablis
*cha gio
challah
chalupa(s)
chamomile
chanterelle
chapati(s)
charbroil
charcuterie
chardonnay
charlotte mold; charlotte russe
charoseth, *see* haroseth
Chartreuse
chateaubriand
chaudfroid
chayote
Cheddar
cheeseburger
cheesecake
cherimoya
cherrystone
Cheshire cheese
chèvre
*chevreuil
*chicharron
chicken-fried steak
chick-pea
chiffonade
chili(es) (*but* chile poblano, chiles rellenos, chile con queso)
chili con carne
chili powder
chili sauce
chimichanga
chine bone
*chinois
chipolata
chipotle
chipped beef
*chiri-mushi
*chirizu
*chiso
*chitarra
*chlodnik
cholent
cholesterol
chopsticks
chorizo(s)
choucroute garnie
*chou-fleur
chowchow
churrasco
cilantro
cinnamon
cioppino
*cipolla
*cipolline
Circassian
clafouti(s)
clambake
clam broth
clamshell
claret
clementine
club sandwich

club soda
Coca-Cola; Coke
cock-a-leekie
coeur à la crème
coffee cake
coffee klatch, *see* kaffeeklatsch
Cognac
Cointreau
colander
colcannon
coleslaw
compote
*concassée
conch(s)
*conchiglie
Concord grapes
confectioners' sugar
confit; confit d'oie
consommé
consommé madrilène
cookie
cookware
coquilles St.-Jacques
corn bread
corn cake
corncob
corn dog
corned beef
cornflakes
corn flour
cornhusk
cornichon
Cornish game hen
cornmeal
corn muffin
corn oil
corn pone
cornstarch
corn syrup
*cotechino
cottage cheese
cottage fries; cottage fried potatoes
coulibiac
*coulis
country captain
country-cured ham
court bouillon
couscous; couscousière
cowpea
*cozze
crab apple
crab cake
crab Louis
crabmeat
cracklings
crayfish (*also, in Louisiana,* crawfish)
Cream of Wheat
cream puff
Crécy
*crema Danica
crème
crème anglaise
crème brûlée
crème de cacao
crème de menthe
crème fraîche
*crème patissière
*cremini
Creole
crepe
crepe(s) suzette
*crespelle
Crisco
crisp-tender

Crock-Pot
croissant
crookneck
*croque madame; croque monsieur
croquembouche
*crostini
croustade
croûte
crouton
crudité(s)
crystallize
*cuchifrito(s)
Cuisinart
cupcake
curaçao
cymling

daikon
daiquiri(s)
dal, *see* dhal
dariole
dasheen
dashi
daube
decaffeinated
deep-fry, deep-fried, deep-frying
deep fryer
déjeuner
*délices
Delicious apple (Golden *and* Red)
Delmonico potatoes, steak
Demerara sugar
*demi-deuil
demi-glace
demitasse
Derby cheese
derma
deviled egg
devil's food cake
dhal
*diavolo
diet Coke, diet Pepsi
dietitian
digestif
Dijon mustard
dijonnaise
dim sum
ditali, ditalini
dolma(s)
*domburi
doughnut
duchesse
*Dugléré
dulse
Dungeness crab
Düsseldorf mustard
Dutch oven
duxelles

eau-de-vie
éclair
écrevisse
eggbeater
Egg Beaters
eggcup

eggdrop soup
egg foo yung
eggnog
egg roll
eggs Benedict
eggshell
*eisbein
Emmentaler
empanada
enchiladas
English muffin
*enokitaki (*also* enoki)
entrecote
entrée
entremets
epazote
*escabeche
escargot(s)
espresso
*estouffade
ethrog
étouffé(e)
extra-virgin olive oil

*fabada asturiana
fagioli
*fajita
falafel
farci(e)
*farfalle
*farfallette
*farfalloni
farfel
farmer cheese
fedelini
*fegatini
feijoada
fenugreek
feta
fettuccelle
fettuccine
fiddlehead fern
Fig Newton
filé powder
filet *(French),* fillet *(English)*
filet(s) mignon(s)
filo, *see* phyllo
fines herbes
finnan haddie
finocchio
fish-and-chips
fish cake
fish fry
fish stick
five-spice powder
flageolet(s)
Flame Tamer
flan(s)
flanken
flank steak
flapjack
flatbread
flatfish
flat-leaf parsley
*flauta
floret
flummery
*focaccia *(sing.),* focacce *(pl.)*
foie gras
fondant
fondue
*fonduta

fontina cheese
forcemeat
fra diavolo
framboise *(the brandy)*
frangipane
freeze-dried, freeze-drying
French dressing
French fries
French toast
*friandises
*fricadelles
fricandeau
fricassee, fricasseed, fricasseeing
Frigidaire
frijole(s)
frittata
frogs' legs
fromage
fruitcake
*fruits de mer *(French),* frutti di mare *(Italian)*
frumenty
fugu
fumet
*funghi trifolati
*fusilli

galantine
galingale
gallimaufry
*galushki *(Ukrainian),* galuska *(Hungarian)*
*ganache
*garam masala
garbanzo(s)
garde-manger
*garganelli
*gastrique
gâteau
gaufre
gaufrette
gazpacho
gefilte fish
gel, *see* jell
gelatin
gelato
*gemelli
*génoise
geoduck
Gewürztraminer
ghee
gherkin
*ghiveci
*giardiera
gigot
ginger ale
gingerbread
gingerroot
gingersnap
ginkgo nut
girasole
*glace de viande
glacé(ed)
glögg
gluhwein
gnocchi
goat's milk
*gohan
Golden Delicious apple
*goma joyu
Gorgonzola

Gouda
*gougère
goujon, goujonette
goulash
grana
granita *(Italian),* granité *(French)*
Granny Smith apple
grappa
gratiné(ed)
gravlax
Great Northern beans
grecque, à la
greengage
*gremolata
*grenouille(s)
griddle cake
grieben
grissini
Gruyère
guacamole
*guasacaca
*güero chili
gugelhupf
*gulyas
gumdrop

Häagen-Dazs
Haas avocado, *see* Hass
haggis
half-and-half
half-moons
half shell
*hallacas
hallah, *see* challah
halvah
hamantasch *(sing.),* hamantaschen *(pl.)*
Hangtown Fry
Hanukkah
hard sauce
hardtack
haricot
hard-shell *(adj.)*
*harissa
haroseth
*harusame
Harvard beets
hasenpfeffer
hash browns, hash brown potatoes
haslet
Hass avocado *(formerly* Haas)
haute cuisine
hazelnut
headcheese
henequen
*herbes de Provence
hero(s)
herring *(sing. and pl.)*
highball
hoecake
hoisin sauce
holishkes
hollandaise
home fries, home fried potatoes
homegrown
homemade
hominy
honeydew melon
hopping John

hors d'oeuvre(s)
horseradish
hotcake
hotchpotch
hot cross buns
hot dog, hot dog roll
howtowdie
Hubbard squash
huevos rancheros
*huitlacoche
*huître
hummus, hummus bi tahini
hush puppy

iceberg lettuce
icebox
ice cream
iced tea
ice water
*imam bayeldi
*impératrice
Indian pudding
insalata mista
involtini

jaggery
jalapeño(s)
jambalaya
*jambon persillé
Jansson's temptation
*jao-tze
jardinière
jell
Jell-O
jelly roll
jerky
Jerusalem artichoke
jicama
johnnycake
*jook soon
Jordan almond
jujube
julienne
junket

kabob, *see* kebab
kaffeeklatsch
Kahlúa
kalamata olive
*käsetorte
kasha
*kasha varnitchkes
*katsuobushi
kebab
kedgeree
kefir
*keftedhes
ketchup
*ketjap manis
Key lime
*kheema
kibbee
kielbasa
Kikkoman

kimchi
king crab
kings' cake
*kinugoshi
Kir
kirsch, kirschwasser
Kitchen Bouquet
KitchenAid
kiwifruit, kiwi
knaidel *(sing.)*, knaidlach *(pl.)*
*knepp
knish
knockwurst
Kobe beef
kohlrabi
kombu
*königsberger klopse
*korma
kosher
koulibiac, *see* coulibiac
kreplach *(sing. and pl.)*
*kritharaki
kuchen
kugel
kugelhopf, *see* gugelhupf
kulich
kümmel
kumquat
kvass

ladyfinger
lamb's-quarter
langouste
langoustine
*laos
lasagna *(a noodle)*
lasagne *(the dish)*
latke(s)
lavash
lazy Susan
leberwurst
lebkuchen
*lefser
leftover
lekvar
lemongrass
lichee, *see* litchi
Liederkranz
Limburger
lingonberry
linguine
*linguine di passeri
linzertorte
lion's head
liptauer
litchi
littleneck clam
lobster Newburg
lobster thermidor
lokshen
*lomi-lomi
London broil
loquat
lox
Lucullan
*luganega
lumpfish
*lussekatter
lutefisk
lychee, *see* litchi
lyonnaise

macadamia nut
*maccheroni
macédoine
mâche
mackerel
Madeira
madeleine
madrilène
*mafalda *(sing.),* mafalde *(pl.)*
*magliette
mahimahi
*mahleb
*mahlepi
maître d'hôtel butter
Malaga
Malakoff
*maltagliati
*mamaliga
mandarin orange
*mandoline
mango(es)
mangosteen
Manhattan clam chowder
Manhattan cocktail
manicotti
manioc
manzanilla
maraschino
marbleize
margarine
margarita
marinara
*marinière
marmalade
marron(s) glacé(s)
marrowbone
marsala
martini(s)
*maruzze
marzipan
masa, masa harina
*mascarpone
matelote
matjes herring
matsutake
matzo(s)
matzo brei
Maui onion
McDonald's
McIntosh apple
Mazola
meatball
meat grinder
meat loaf
Médoc
*mee krob
*mehlsuppe
*melanzane
melba sauce
melba toast
*ménagère
menudo
mesclun
*metzelsuppe
meunière
Meursault
*meze, mezedaki
*mezzani
milk shake
mille-feuille(s)
*millefoglie
minestrone
Minute rice
mirabelle
mirepoix
*mirin
mirliton
*miroton

miso
Mixmaster
*mizutaki
Moët et Chandon
mole
mollusk
*mondongo
monkfish
monosodium glutamate, MSG
Monterey Jack
Montrachet
*moo-shu
*morcilla
morel
Mornay sauce
mortadella
*mostaccioli
*mostarda di frutta
moussaka
mozzarella
*mozzarella in carrozza
Muenster
*mu-er
*muffuletta
mulligan stew
mulligatawny
Muscovy duck
*mushimono
muskmelon

napoleon
*nasi goreng
*natto
navarin
navy bean
Nescafé
Nesselrode
Neufchâtel
Newburg
*ngah choy
niçoise
*nigiri-sushi
*nimono
*nishime
nockerl *(sing.)*, nockerln *(pl.)*
noisette
nonalcoholic
nonaluminum
noncorrosive
nondairy
nonmetallic
nonoily
nonreactive
nonstick
nopal
nori
*norimaki
nouvelle cuisine
*nuoc mam
NutraSweet

*naan
*nabemomo
*nameko
*nam pla
napa cabbage

O'Brien potatoes
*oeufs à la neige
offal
old-fashioned *(the cocktail)*

omelet *(American),* omelette *(French)*
open-face sandwich
*oreganata
oregano
orgeat
Orlov (*also* Orloff)
*orrechiette
ortolan
orzo
osso buco
ovenproof
*oursin
ouzo

*pad thai
paella
*paglia e fieno
paillard
*pain perdu
*pakora
*palmier
panada
panbroil
*pancetta
pandowdy
pan dulce
panettone
panfry
papillote
*pappadam
*pappardelle
*paprikash
parboil, parcook
Parker House rolls
Parmesan
parmigiana
Parmigiano-Reggiano
parsleyed
*pasilla
paskha
passion fruit
*pasta all' uovo
*pasta asciutta
*pasta e fagiole
*pasta fresca
*pasticceria
pasticcio *(Italian),* pastitsio *(Greek)*
pâte *(the pastry)*
pâté *(terrine)*
pâte à choux
*pâte brisée
pâté de foie gras
*pâte feuilletée
patisserie
patna rice
pattypan
paupiettes
pease pudding
pêche melba
pecorino
Peking duck
pelmeni
pemmican
*penne
*peperoncini
peperoni *(chili)*
pepperoni *(sausage)*
pepper pot
*pequin chili
*perche-pierres
*perciatelli
Périgord

Pernod
Persian melon
persillade
*pescado
pesto
petit(s) four(s)
petite marmite
petits pois
pe-tsai
*pfannkuchen
pfefferkuchen
pheasant *(sing. and pl.)*
*pho
phyllo
*picadillo
piccalilli
piccata
pièce de résistance
piecrust
pignolia
pilaf
pimento cheese
pimiento(s)
piña colada
pine nut
*pipérade
piripiri
piroshki
*pissaladière
*pisto
*pistou
pita
*pithiviers
*pizzaiola
*plaki
plantain
plátano(s)
*pleurotes
*poblano
poi
*poisson
poivrade
*Pojarski
*pok-choi
polenta
*polipo
pollo
*polpette
*polpettine
*polpettone
pomegranate
*pomme(s) de terre
Pont l'Évêque
*ponzu
poori, *see* puri
poor knights of Windsor
popover
*poppadum, *see* pappadam
poppy seed
porcini
Port Salut
port wine
posole
potato chip
potatoes Anna
pot-au-feu
pot cheese
*potée
potherb
potpie
pot roast
pottage
poularde
*poule au pot
poulette sauce
pound cake
pozole, *see* posole

prebaked, precook, preground, preheat
*pré-salé
primavera
process cheese
profiterole
prosciutto
provençal(e)
provolone
*ptcha
puffballs
pumpernickel
pupu
purée, puréed, puréeing
puri
*puttanesca
Pyrex

*quadrettini
quahog
quail *(sing. and pl.)*
*quatre épices
quenelle
quesadilla
quetsch
quiche lorraine
quick bread
quinoa

raclette
radicchio
ragout
*ragù
*raita
ramekin
rape, *see* broccoli rape
rascasse
ratatouille
ravigote
ravioli
Reblochon
réchauffé
redeye gravy
red snapper
rémoulade
retsina
Reuben sandwich
*Ricard
ricotta
Riesling
rigatoni
rijsttafel
rillettes
*ris de veau
*risi e bisi
risotto
rissole *(n.)*, rissolé *(adj.)*
*rivvels
Rock Cornish game hen
rockfish
rock lobster
*rødkaal
rollmops *(sing. and pl.)*
romaine
Romano
*romescu
root beer
Roquefort
rose hips
rose water

*rösti
*rotelle
*rotini
roughy
rouille
roulades *(French),* rouladen *(German)*
roux
*rugelach
rumaki
Russian dressing
rutabaga

sabayon
saccharin
Sacher torte
Saint-Honoré
sake
salami
Salisbury steak
Sally Lunn
salmagundi
salmi
salsa
*salsa verde
saltfish
saltimbocca
saltine
saltwater
sambuca
samphire
sangría
sapodilla
sapsago
*sarmi
sashimi
saté (*also* satay)
saucisson
sauerbraten
sauté, sautéed, sautéing
Sauternes *(French),* sauterne *(American)*
sauvignon blanc
savarin
savory
savoy cabbage
scaloppine
scampi
schav
schlag
schmaltz
schnapps
schnecke *(sing.),* schnecken *(pl.)*
schnitz and knepp
schnitzel
Scotch woodcock
scungilli
seafood
seashell
Seckel pear
seder
seedcake
semisweet
semolina
*serrano(s)
sesame oil
seviche
Seville orange
*sevruga
*sfogliatelle
*shabu shabu
*shao-hsing wine
shark's fin soup

shashlik
shellfish
shepherd's pie
sherbet
sherry
shiitake
*shinsonro
*shiru
shish kebab
*shiu mai
shoofly pie
shortbread
shortcake
short ribs
shoyu
shrimp(s)
Sichuan (formerly Szechwan)
SilverStone
*skordalia
slivovitz
slumgullion
smorgasbord
smørrebrød
*soba
soffrito *(Italian),* sofrito *(Spanish)*
soft-boiled
soft-cooked
soft-shell *(adj.)*
sommelier
sopaipilla
*sopa seca
sorbet
soubise
soufflé, souffléed
soul food
soupbone
soupçon
soupspoon
sour cream
sourdough
soursop
sous-chef
souvlakia
soybean
spaetzle *or* spätzle
*spanakopitta
Spanish rice
spareribs
*spiedini
sponge cake
spoon bread
springform pan
spumone
squab(s)
star anise
steak and kidney pie
steak tartare
*stifado
Stilton
stingaree
stir-fry
stockpot
stollen *(sing. and pl.)*
stone-ground
store-bought
stove-top *(adj.)*
*stracchino
*stracciatella
streusel
string bean
stroganoff
succotash
sugarplum
sugar snap pea
*sugo

*suimono
sukiyaki
sunchoke
*sunomono
superfine sugar
suprême
*surumi
sushi
sweet-and-sour *(adj.)*
sweetbreads
Sweet 'n Low
Swiss chard
Swiss cheese
Swiss steak
syllabub
syrup
Szechwan, *see* Sichuan
*szekely goulash

Tabasco
tabbouleh
taco(s)
*tagine
tagliarini
tagliatelle
tahini
*takinoko
tamale
*tamari
tandoori
tangelo
tapa(s)
*tapenade
*tarama, taramasalata
*tarka
taro
tartar sauce
*tarte Tatin
T-bone steak
Teflon
teiglach
tempura
*teppanyaki
tequila
teriyaki
tetrazzini
Thermidor
Thousand Island dressing
*tikka murgh
*tikki kabob
Tilsit cheese
timbale
*tiramisù
*tiropetes
tisane
toad-in-the-hole
tofu
Toll-House
tomalley
tomatillo(s)
*tonkatsu
*tonnato
*tonno
topinambour
tortellini
tortilla
tostada
*tostones
tournedos *(sing. and pl.)*
tourtière
treacle
tree ears

*trenette
Triple Sec
*truite au bleu
*tsukemono
*tubetti
*tubettini
*tufoli
*tuile
tuna fish
turk's-head pan
turmeric
tuscarora rice
tutti-frutti
tzimmes

*uccelletti
*udon
ugli fruit
underripe, undercooked
*unido
unsulfured
upside-down cake
*usli ghee

*vacherin
vanilla bean
vanilla extract
*vareniki
*varnitchkes
V-8 juice
velouté
verjuice
vermicelli
vermouth
Véronique
*vesiga, *see* viziga
vichyssoise
Vidalia onion
*vindaloo
*vitello tonnato
*viziga
vol-au-vent(s)

*wakame
Waldorf salad
Walla Walla onion
walleyed pike
wasabi
watercress
waterzooi
weakfish
*weisswurst
Welsh rabbit
Wensleydale
whiskey *(American),* whisky *(Scotch, Irish, Canadian)*
whitebait
whitefish
whole wheat flour
Wiener schnitzel
wienerwurst
wineglass
witloof
wonton

wood ears
Worcestershire sauce

*yakimono
yakitori
yautia
yellowfin
yogurt
Yorkshire pudding
*yosenabe

zabaglione
*zampone
*zarzuela
*zensai
Ziploc
ziti
zucchini
zuppa di pesce
zuppa inglese
zwieback

Suggested Reference Books

Among the many cookbooks available as sources of recipes, some are invaluable as reference books for writers and editors. The following are books we refer to frequently—for definitions, spelling of foreign words, descriptions of techniques and procedures, and other useful information.

Food Dictionaries and Encyclopedias

A Concise Encyclopedia of Gastronomy, by André L. Simon (Woodstock, N.Y.: Overlook, 1981).

The Cook Book, by Terence and Caroline Conran (New York: Crown, 1980).

Cooking A to Z: The Complete Culinary Reference Tool, edited by Jane Horn (San Francisco: California Culinary Academy, 1992).

The Cook's Encyclopedia: Ingredients and Processes, by Tom Stobart (New York: HarperCollins, 1981).

Cook's Ingredients, Adrian Bailey, contributing editor (Pleasantville, N.Y.: Reader's Digest Association, 1990).

Craig Claiborne's The New York Times Food Encyclopedia, by Craig Claiborne (New York: Times Books, 1985).

Food Lover's Companion, by Sharon Tyler Herbst (New York: Barron's, 1990).

Larousse Gastronomique, edited by Jenifer Harvey Lang (new American edition) (New York: Crown, 1988).

Menu Mystique: The Diner's Guide to Fine Food and Drink, by Norman Odya Krohn (Middle Village, N.Y.: Jonathan David, 1983).

Le Répertoire de la Cuisine, by Louis Saulnier (text edition) (New York: Barron's, 1977).

General Cookbooks

The Art of Cooking, Volumes I and II, by Jacques Pépin (paperback edition) (New York: Knopf, 1992).

The Family Circle Cookbook, by editors of *Family Circle* and David Ricketts (New York: Simon and Schuster, 1992).

The Fannie Farmer Cookbook, revised by Marion Cunningham with Jeri Laber (new edition) (New York: Knopf, 1990).

Joy of Cooking, by Irma S. Rombauer and Marion Rombauer Becker (New York: Bobbs-Merrill, 1975).

The New Doubleday Cookbook, by Jean Anderson and Elaine Hanna (New York: Doubleday, 1985; paperback edition, 1990).

The New James Beard, by James Beard (New York: Knopf, 1981).

The New York Times Cook Book, by Craig Claiborne (revised edition) (New York: HarperCollins, 1990).

The Way to Cook, by Julia Child (New York: Knopf, 1989).

Specialized Cookbooks

Chef Paul Prudhomme's Louisiana Kitchen, by Paul Prudhomme (New York: Morrow, 1984).

Cuisine of the American Southwest, by Anne Lindsay Greer (Greenwich, Conn.: Cuisinart Cooking Club, 1983).

The Encyclopedia of Fish Cookery, by A. J. McClane (New York: Holt, 1977).

Fresh Food, edited by Sylvia Rosenthal (New York: Dutton, 1978).

The International Kosher Cookbook, by the 92nd Street Y Kosher Cooking School, edited by Batia Plotch and Patricia Kobe (New York: Fawcett, 1992).

Maida Heatter's Book of Great Desserts, by Maida Heatter (revised edition) (New York: Knopf, 1991).

Microwave Gourmet, by Barbara Kafka (New York: Morrow, 1987).

The New Complete Book of Breads, by Bernard Clayton, Jr. (New York: Simon and Schuster, 1987).

The New Complete Book of Pasta, by Maria Luisa Scott and Jack Denton Scott (New York: Morrow, 1985).

Uncommon Fruits and Vegetables: A Commonsense Guide, by Elizabeth Schneider (New York: HarperCollins, 1986).

Foreign Cuisines

Asia and Far East

An American Taste of Japan, by Elizabeth Andoh (New York: Morrow, 1985).

The Chinese Cookbook, by Craig Claiborne and Virginia Lee (paperback edition) (New York: HarperCollins, 1983).

Chinese Technique, by Ken Hom with Harvey Steiman (New York: Simon and Schuster, 1981).

Classic Indian Cooking, by Julie Sahni (New York: Morrow, 1980).

The Cuisines of Asia, by Jennifer Brennan (New York: St. Martin's/Marek, 1984; paperback edition, 1989).

Foods of Vietnam, by Nicole Routhier (New York: Stewart, Tabori & Chang, 1989).

Madhur Jaffrey's Indian Cooking, by Madhur Jaffrey (paperback edition) (New York: Barron's, 1983).

The Simple Art of Vietnamese Cooking, by Binh Duong and Marcia Kiesel (New York: Prentice Hall Press, 1991).

Europe and Russia

FRANCE

The Escoffier Cook Book: A Guide to the Fine Art of French Cuisine, by Auguste Escoffier (New York: Crown, 1969).

Mastering the Art of French Cooking, Volume I, by Julia Child, Louisette Bertholle, and Simone Beck (New York: Knopf, 1961); Volume II, by Julia Child and Simone Beck (New York: Knopf, 1970).

GERMANY

The Cuisines of Germany, by Horst Scharfenberg (New York: Poseidon, 1989).

GREECE

The Complete Book of Greek Cooking, by the Recipe Club of St. Paul's Greek Orthodox Cathedral (New York: HarperCollins, 1990; HarperPerennial, 1991).

The Food and Wine of Greece, by Diane Kochilas (New York: St. Martin's, 1990).

ITALY

The Essentials of Classic Italian Cooking, by Marcella Hazan (New York: Knopf, 1992).

The Fine Art of Italian Cooking, by Giuliano Bugialli (New York: Times Books, 1989).

Italian Cooking in the Grand Tradition, by Jo Bettoja and Anna Maria Cornetto (New York: Simon and Schuster, 1982; Fireside, 1991).

POLAND

The Art of Polish Cooking, by Alina Zeranska (New York: Pelican, 1989).

PORTUGAL

The Food of Portugal, by Jean Anderson (New York: Morrow, 1986).

RUSSIA

The Art of Russian Cuisine, by Anne Volokh with Mavis Manus (New York: Macmillan, 1983; paperback, 1989).

A Taste of Russia (originally *À la Russe*), by Darra Goldstein (New York: HarperPerennial, 1991).

Spain

The Foods and Wines of Spain, by Penelope Casas (New York: Knopf, 1984).

Tapas: The Little Dishes of Spain, by Penelope Casas (New York: Knopf, 1991).

Mexico and South America

The Art of South American Cooking, by Felipe Rojas-Lombardi (New York: HarperCollins, 1991).

The Cuisines of Mexico, by Diana Kennedy (New York: HarperCollins, 1986; HarperPerennial, 1989).

Index